HOLT 3 FRENCH

Allez, viens! ®

Student Make-Up Assignments

D1273660

HOLT, RINEHART AND WINSTON

A Harcourt Classroom Education Company

Austin · New York · Orlando · Atlanta · San Francisco · Boston · Dallas · Toronto · London

Contributing Writer

Isabelle Cate
Austin, TX

Cover Photo Credits
(tl), Tim Haske/Index Stock; (tr), Network Production/Index Stock (b) Digital Imagery® ©2003 Photodisc, Inc.

Art Credits
All art, unless otherwise noted, by Holt, Rinehart & Winston.

ALLEZ, VIENS! is a trademark licensed to Holt, Rinehart and Winston, registered in the United States of America and/or other jurisdictions.

Printed in the United States of America

ISBN 0-03-065687-7

3 4 5 6 7 8   023   07 06 05 04

Table of Contents

ANSWERS

Holt French 3 Allez, viens!

To the Teacher

The blackline masters in this ancillary will help you keep track of the instructional material covered in a school year, so that you can give make-up information to students who missed class.

The first section of the book is a Diagnostic Table. In the first column of the table is a list of all the major presentations that make up the building blocks of the **Chapitre**: the functional expressions, the grammar, and the vocabulary. The activities listed in the other four columns are correlated to the **Grammaire supplémentaire** in the *Pupil's Edition,* the **Cahier d'activités**, the **Travaux pratiques de grammaire,** and the **Interactive CD-ROM Tutor.** This table, which gives you an overview of the presentations and opportunities for practice, can also be used as a global reference for students who need extra practice in problem areas.

The second section of the book contains the Student Make-Up Assignments Checklists. These blackline masters (one for each **étape** of the *Pupil's Edition*) can be photocopied and given to students as make-up assignments. On the left-hand side of each blackline master is a list of the presentations in each **étape.** If students missed a specific presentation (or presentations), the checklist tells them what activities they can do in the **Grammaire supplémentaire** in the *Pupil's Edition,* the **Cahier d'activités**, the **Travaux pratiques de grammaire,** or the **Interactive CD-ROM Tutor** to practice the material they missed when they were absent from class.

The third section of the book contains Alternative Quizzes that can be given to students who were absent from class when the regular Grammar and Vocabulary Quiz (Quiz A in the Testing Program) was given. The Alternative Quizzes could also be used in a different way: You can give both quizzes in the regular class, alternating rows, for example, so that students are not tempted to glance at their neighbor's paper.

The Alternative Quizzes were carefully built to reflect the same weight and level of difficulty as the regular quizzes, so that you can be assured that two students who take different versions of the quiz feel that they have been tested equally.

Diagnostic Information

The activities listed in this table are taken from the **Grammaire supplémentaire** in the *Pupil's Edition*, the **Cahier d'activités,** the **Travaux pratiques de grammaire,** and the **Interactive CD-ROM Tutor.** They provide students with extra practice in problem areas.

Grammaire = white background; **Vocabulaire** = light gray; **Comment dit-on…?** = dark gray

CHAPITRE 1	Grammaire supplémentaire	Travaux pratiques de grammaire	Cahier d'activités	Interactive CD-ROM Tutor
Renewing old acquaintances			Act. 2, p. 2	
Inquiring; expressing enthusiasm and dissatisfaction			Act. 3, p. 2	
Exchanging information			Act. 5, p. 3	Act. 1, CD 1
The **passé composé**	Acts. 1–3, pp. 24–25	Acts. 1–4, pp. 1–3	Act. 6, p.4	Act. 2, CD 1
Asking and describing what a place was like			Act. 7, p. 4	
The **imparfait**	Acts. 4–5, p. 25	Acts. 5–8, pp. 4–5	Act. 8, p. 5	Act. 3, CD 1
Expressing indecision; making recommendations			Act. 11, p. 7	Act. 4, CD 1
Vocabulaire: French menu items		Acts. 9–11, pp. 6–7	Acts. 12–13, p. 8	
Ordering and asking for details		Acts. 12–13, p. 8	Act. 15, p. 9	Acts. 5–6, CD 1

CHAPITRE 2	Grammaire supplémentaire	Travaux pratiques de grammaire	Cahier d'activités	Interactive CD-ROM Tutor
Asking for and giving directions		Act. 1, p. 9	Acts. 2–3, pp. 14–15	Act. 2, CD 1
Vocabulaire: at the gas station		Acts. 2–3, p. 10	Act. 4, p. 15	Act. 1, CD 1
The verb **conduire**	Act. 2, p. 54	Act. 4, p. 11	Act. 6, p. 16	
Expressing impatience; reassuring someone			Act. 7, p. 16	
The imperative	Acts. 3–6, pp. 54–55	Acts. 5–7, pp. 11–12	Act. 9, p. 17	Act. 3, CD 1
Expressing enthusiasm and boredom			Act. 12, p. 19	
Vocabulaire: adjectives to express enthusiasm and boredom		Acts. 8–9, pp. 13–14	Act. 13, p. 19	Act. 4, CD 1
Pronouns and their placement	Acts. 7–11, pp. 55–57	Acts. 10–15, pp. 14–17	Acts. 15–16, pp. 20–21	Act. 5, CD 1
Asking and telling where things are			Act. 18, p. 22	Act. 6, CD 1

CHAPITRE 3	Grammaire supplémentaire	Travaux pratiques de grammaire	Cahier d'activités	Interactive CD-ROM Tutor
Vocabulaire: household chores		Acts. 1–4, pp. 18–19	Acts. 2–3, p. 26	Act. 1, CD 1
Asking for, granting, and refusing permission; expressing obligation	Acts. 1–2, p. 84	Acts. 5–6, p. 20	Act. 5, p. 27	Acts. 2–3, CD 1
The subjunctive	Acts. 3–6, pp. 85–86	Acts. 7–15, pp. 21–25	Acts. 7–8, p. 28	Act. 4, CD 1
Vocabulaire: personal responsibilities		Acts. 16–17, p. 26	Act. 9, p. 29	
Forbidding		Act. 22, p. 28		
Negative with infinitives	Acts. 7–9, pp. 86–87	Acts. 18–19, p. 27		Act. 5, CD 1
Vocabulaire: social responsibilities		Acts. 20–22, p. 28	Act. 14, p. 31	Act. 6, CD 1
Reproaching; justifying your actions; rejecting others' excuses			Acts. 16–18, pp. 32–33	
CHAPITRE 4	Grammaire supplémentaire	Travaux pratiques de grammaire	Cahier d'activités	Interactive CD-ROM Tutor
Vocabulaire: clothing		Acts. 1–7, pp. 29–32	Acts. 2–3, p. 38	Act. 1, CD 1
Asking for and giving opinions			Act. 4, p. 38	Act. 2, CD 1
Vocabulaire: adjectives for clothing		Acts. 8–12, pp. 32–34	Act. 5, p. 39	
Asking which one(s); pointing out and identifying people and things			Act. 7, p. 40	
The interrogative and demonstrative pronouns	Acts. 1–3, pp. 114–115	Acts. 13–17, pp. 35–37	Act. 8, p. 40	Act. 3, CD 1
Vocabulaire: hair and hairstyles		Acts. 18–21, pp. 38–39	Acts. 12–15, pp. 43–44	Act. 4, CD 1
The causative faire	Acts. 4, 6–7, pp. 116–117	Acts. 22–23, p. 40	Act. 16, p. 45	Act. 5, CD 1
Paying and responding to compliments; reassuring someone	Act. 5, p. 116		Acts. 17–20, pp. 45–46	Act. 6, CD 1

Holt French 3 Allez, viens!

CHAPITRE 5	Grammaire supplémentaire	Travaux pratiques de grammaire	Cahier d'activités	Interactive CD-ROM Tutor
Vocabulaire: choices and plans		Acts. 1–4, pp. 41–42	Act. 3, p. 50	Act. 1, CD 2
Asking about and expressing intentions; expressing conditions and possibilities		Acts. 5–7, pp. 43–44	Acts. 4–6, pp. 50–51	
The future	Acts. 2–4, pp. 148–149	Acts. 8–13, pp. 45–48	Acts. 8–9, p. 52	Act. 2, CD 2
Vocabulaire: careers		Acts. 14–17, pp. 49–50	Acts. 13–14, p. 55	Act. 3, CD 2
Asking about future plans; expressing wishes; expressing indecision; giving advice			Acts. 15–16, pp. 55–56	Act. 4, CD 2
The conditional	Acts. 5–7, pp. 150–151	Acts. 18–20, pp. 51–52	Acts. 17–19, pp. 56–57	Act. 5, CD 2
Requesting information; writing a formal letter			Act. 21, p. 58	Act. 6, CD 2
Inversion	Acts. 8–9, p. 151	Act. 21, p. 53		

CHAPITRE 6	Grammaire supplémentaire	Travaux pratiques de grammaire	Cahier d'activités	Interactive CD-ROM Tutor
Making, accepting, and refusing suggestions			Act. 2, p. 62	Act. 2, CD 2
Making arrangements			Act. 4, p. 62	Act. 2, CD 2
Reciprocal verbs	Acts. 1–2, p. 178	Acts. 1–7, pp. 54–57	Acts. 5–6, p. 63	Act. 1, CD 2
Making and accepting apologies			Act. 8, p. 64	Act. 2, CD 2
The past infinitive	Act. 3, p. 179	Acts. 8–11, pp. 58–59	Act. 9, p. 65	Act. 3, CD 2
Showing and responding to hospitality; expressing and responding to thanks	Act. 4, p. 179		Act. 12, p. 67	Act. 4, CD 2
Vocabulaire: family members		Acts. 12–17, pp. 60–62	Acts. 13–14, pp. 68–69	Act. 5, CD 2
Quarreling	Acts. 5–7, pp. 180–181		Acts. 15–17, p. 70	Act. 6, CD 2

CHAPITRE 7	Grammaire supplémentaire	Travaux pratiques de grammaire	Cahier d'activités	Interactive CD-ROM Tutor
Vocabulaire: rain forest and savanna		Acts. 1–3, pp. 63–64	Act. 2, p. 74	Act. 1, CD 2
Making suppositions; expressing doubt and certainty			Act. 3, pp. 74–75	Act. 3, CD 2
When to use the subjunctive		Act. 4, pp. 64–65		
Vocabulaire: packing for a safari		Acts. 5–6, pp. 65–66	Act. 4, p. 75	Act. 2, CD 2
Asking for and giving advice			Act. 5, p. 75	Act. 3, CD 2
Using the subjunctive	Acts. 2–4, pp. 208–209	Acts. 7–9, pp. 66–68	Act. 6, p. 76	Act. 4, CD 2
Vocabulaire: African animals		Acts. 10–11, p. 69	Acts. 10–11, pp. 79–80	Act. 5, CD 2
Expressing astonishment			Act. 12, p. 81	
Cautioning someone; expressing fear; reassuring someone; expressing relief		Acts. 12–13, p. 70	Act. 13, p. 81	
Irregular subjunctive forms	Acts. 5–8, pp. 210–21	Acts. 14–16, pp. 71–72	Act. 14, p. 82	Act. 6, CD 2

CHAPITRE 8	Grammaire supplémentaire	Travaux pratiques de grammaire	Cahier d'activités	Interactive CD-ROM Tutor
Asking someone to convey good wishes; closing a letter			Act. 2, p. 86	Act. 1, CD 2
Vocabulaire: traditional life		Acts. 1–3, pp. 73–74	Acts. 3–5, pp. 86–87	Act. 2, CD 2
Expressing hopes or wishes; giving advice	Act. 2, p. 238			
Si clauses	Acts. 2–5, pp. 238–240	Acts. 4–9, pp. 74–77	Acts. 6–7, p. 88	Act. 3, CD 2
Vocabulaire: city life		Acts. 10–13, pp. 78–79	Act. 13, p. 91	Act. 4, CD 2
Complaining; expressing annoyance			Acts. 14–15, p. 92	
Making comparisons			Act. 16, p. 93	Act. 5, CD 2
The comparative	Acts. 6–9, pp. 240–241	Acts. 14–16, pp. 80–81	Acts. 17–18, pp. 93–94	Act. 6, CD 2

CHAPITRE 9	Grammaire supplémentaire	Travaux pratiques de grammaire	Cahier d'activités	Interactive CD-ROM Tutor
Vocabulaire: television programming		Acts. 1–4, pp. 82–83	Act. 2, p. 98	Act. 1, CD 3
Agreeing and disagreeing; expressing indifference			Act. 4, p. 99	Act. 3, CD 3
Vocabulaire: the television		Acts. 5–6, p. 84	Acts. 5–6, pp. 99–100	
Negative expressions	Acts. 1–3, pp. 272–273	Acts. 7–9, pp. 85–86	Act. 7, p. 100	Act. 2, CD 3
Ne...que	Act. 4, p. 273	Act. 10, p. 86		
Making requests			Act. 9, p. 101	Act. 3, CD 3
Vocabulaire: types of movies		Act. 11, p. 87	Acts. 12–13, p. 103	Act. 4, CD 3
Asking for and making judgments; asking for and making recommendations			Act. 14, p. 104	Act. 6, CD 3
Asking about and summarizing a story			Act. 15, p. 105	Act. 6, CD 3
Relative pronouns	Acts. 5–9, pp. 273–275	Acts. 12–13, pp. 87–88	Acts. 16–17, pp. 105–106	Act. 5, CD 3
CHAPITRE 10	Grammaire supplémentaire	Travaux pratiques de grammaire	Cahier d'activités	Interactive CD-ROM Tutor
Vocabulaire: sea life		Acts. 1–2, p. 89	Acts. 2–3, p. 110	Act. 1, CD 3
Bragging; flattering			Acts. 4–5, p. 111	Act. 3, CD 3
The superlative	Acts. 1–4, pp. 302–303	Acts. 3–7, pp. 90–92	Acts. 6–7, pp. 111–112	Act. 2, CD 3
Teasing			Acts. 9–10, p. 113	Act. 3, CD 3
Vocabulaire: everyday life		Acts. 8–9, p. 93	Acts. 12–13, p. 115	Act. 4, CD 3
Breaking some news; showing interest; expressing disbelief			Act. 14, p. 116	Act. 5, CD 3
The past perfect	Acts. 5–6, pp. 304–305	Acts. 10–12, pp. 94–95	Acts. 16–17, p. 117	Act. 6, CD 3
Telling a joke	Act. 7, p. 305		Act. 19, p. 118	

CHAPITRE 11	Grammaire supplémentaire	Travaux pratiques de grammaire	Cahier d'activités	Interactive CD-ROM Tutor
Asking for confirmation	Acts. 2–3, p. 332		Acts. 2–3, p. 122	
Vocabulaire: music and musical instruments		Acts. 1–4, pp. 96–97	Acts. 4–5, p. 123	Act. 1, CD 3
Asking for and giving opinions; agreeing and disagreeing			Acts. 6–8, pp. 124–125	Act. 2, CD 3
Asking for explanations	Acts. 4–5, p. 333		Act. 10, p. 127	
Vocabulaire: Cajun food	Act. 6, p. 334	Acts. 5–9, pp. 98–100	Acts. 11–15, pp. 127–129	Acts. 3–4, CD 3
Making observations; giving impressions	Acts. 8–10, pp. 334–335	Acts. 10–12, pp. 100–101	Acts. 16–17, p. 130	Acts. 5–6, CD 3
CHAPITRE 12	Grammaire supplémentaire	Travaux pratiques de grammaire	Cahier d'activités	Interactive CD-ROM Tutor
Vocabulaire: sports and equipment		Acts. 1–5, pp. 102–103	Acts. 2–4, pp. 134–135	Act. 1, CD 3
Expressing anticipation; making suppositions; expressing certainty and doubt			Acts. 6–7, p. 136	Act. 2, CD 3
The future after **quand** and **dès que**	Acts. 2–5, pp. 360–361	Acts. 6–7, p. 104	Act. 8, p. 137	Act. 3, CD 3
Vocabulaire: places of origin	Acts. 6–8, pp. 362–363	Acts. 8–13, pp.105–107	Act. 11, p. 139	Act. 4, CD 3
Inquiring			Acts. 12–13, pp. 140–141	Act. 5, CD 3
Expressing excitement and disappointment			Acts. 14–15, pp. 141–142	Act. 6, CD 3

Holt French 3 Allez, viens!

Student Make-Up Assignments Checklist

France, les régions

■ PREMIERE ETAPE Student Make-Up Assignments Checklist

Pupil's Edition, pp. 9–11

Study the expressions in the **Comment dit–on…?** box on page 9: renewing old acquaintances. You should know how to greet someone you haven't seen recently.	☐ Do Activity 9, p. 9. Write the conversation between you and a friend you haven't seen in a year. ☐ For additional practice, do Activity 2, p. 2 in the **Cahier d'activités**.
Study the expressions in the **Comment dit–on…?** box on page 9: inquiring; expressing enthusiasm and dissatisfaction. You should know how to inquire about someone's trip or vacation, and how to express enthusiasm and dissatisfaction.	☐ Do Activity 11, p. 10 as a writing activity. ☐ For additional practice, do Activity 3, p. 2 in the **Cahier d'activités**.
Study the expressions in the **Comment dit–on…?** box on page 10: exchanging information. You should know how to ask about someone's trip or vacation, and how to answer such questions.	☐ Do Activity 12, p. 10 as a writing activity. ☐ For additional practice, do Activity 5, p. 3 in the **Cahier d'activités**. ☐ For additional practice, do Activity 1, CD 1 in the **Interactive CD–ROM Tutor**.
Study the grammar presentation in the **Grammaire** box on page 11: the **passé composé**.	☐ Do Activity 14, p. 12 as a writing acitvity. ☐ For additional practice, do Activities 1–3, pp. 24–25 in the **Grammaire supplémentaire**. ☐ For additional practice, do Activities 1–4, pp. 1–3 in the **Travaux Pratiques de Grammaire**. ☐ For additional practice, do Activity 6, p. 4 in the **Cahier d'activités**. ☐ For additional practice, do Activity 2, CD 1 in the **Interactive CD–ROM Tutor**.

CHAPITRE 1

■ PREMIERE ETAPE Student Make-Up Assignments Checklist

Pupil's Edition, pp. 12–13

Study the expressions in the **Comment dit–on...?** box on page 12: asking and describing what a place was like. You should know how to ask what a place was like and how to describe what a place was like.	☐ Do Activity 7, p. 4 in the **Cahier d'activités.**
Study the grammar presentation in the **Grammaire** box on page 13: the **imparfait.**	☐ Do Activity 16, p. 13 as a writing activity. ☐ Do Activity 17, p. 13 as a writing activity. ☐ For additional practice, do Activities 4–5, p. 25 in the **Grammaire supplémentaire.** ☐ For additional practice, do Activities 5–8, pp. 4–5 in the **Travaux pratiques de grammaire.** ☐ For additional practice, do Activity 8, p. 5 in the **Cahier d'activités.** ☐ For additional practice, do Activity 3, CD 1 in the **Interactive CD–ROM Tutor.**

■ PREMIERE ETAPE Self-Test

Can you renew old acquaintances?	How would you...
	1. greet a friend you hadn't seen in a while?
	2. inquire about your friend's activities?
	How would you respond if...
	1. a friend you hadn't seen in a while greeted you?
	2. your friend wanted to know what you've been doing?
Can you inquire and express enthusiasm and dissatisfaction?	How would you ask a friend how his or her vacation was?
	How might these people describe their vacations?
	1. Sylvie went to Hawaii but it rained all week.
	2. Hervé went camping and a bear broke into his tent.
	3. Brigitte and Céline went to Paris.
	4. Julie water–skied all summer.
Can you exchange information?	What questions would you ask to find out...
	1. where your friend went on vacation.
	2. how he or she got there.
	3. who he or she went with.
	4. where he or she stayed.
	5. what the weather was like.
	How would you answer these same questions?
Can you ask and describe what a place was like?	How would you ask what a place was like?
	How would you describe a place?

 For an online self-test, go to **go.hrw.com**.

WA3 FRANCOPHONE EUROPE–1

1 France, les régions

■ DEUXIEME ETAPE Student Make-Up Assignments Checklist

Pupil's Edition, pp. 17–18

Study the expressions in the **Comment dit–on...?** box on page 17: expressing indecision; making recommendations. You should know what to say when undecided on what to order at a restaurant, and how to recommend a dish to someone.	☐ Do Activity 11, p. 7 in the **Cahier d'activités**. ☐ For additional practice, do Activity 4, CD 1 in the **Interactive CD–ROM Tutor**.
Study the **Vocabulaire** on page 17.	☐ Do Activity 29, p. 18 as a writing activity. ☐ For additional practice, do Activities 9–11, pp. 6–7 in the **Travaux Pratiques de Grammaire**. ☐ For additional practice, do Activities 12–13, p. 8 in the **Cahier d'activités**.

■ DEUXIEME ETAPE Student Make-Up Assignments Checklist

Pupil's Edition, pp. 18–19

Study the expressions in the **Comment dit–on...?** box on page 18: ordering and asking for details. You should know how to order at a restaurant and how to ask for details about the menu or a dish. You should also know how the waiter can answer your questions.

☐ Do Activity 31, p. 19 as a writing activity.

☐ Do Activity 32, p. 19 as a writing activity.

☐ For additional practice, do Activities 12–13, p. 8 in the **Travaux Pratiques de Grammaire.**

☐ For additional practice, do Activity 15, p. 9 in the **Cahier d'activités.**

☐ For additional practice, do Activities 5–6, CD 1 in the **Interactive CD–ROM.**

CHAPITRE 1

■ DEUXIEME ETAPE Self-Test

Can you express indecision?	What would you say if you couldn't decide what to order in a restaurant?
Can you make recommendations?	How would you recommend that someone order a certain dish? How would you ask the server… 1. what the restaurant's specialties are? 2. what kinds of appetizers there are? 3. What he recommands?
Can you order and ask for details?	How would you order each of the following items? 1. un café 2. du poulet 3. de la glace aux fraises

 For an online self-test, go to **go.hrw.com**.

WA3 FRANCOPHONE EUROPE–1

CHAPITRE 2

Belgique, nous voilà!

■ PREMIERE ETAPE Student Make-Up Assignments Checklist

Pupil's Edition, pp. 37–40

Study the expressions in the **Comment dit–on…?** box on page 37: asking for and giving directions. You should know how to ask for directions and give directions.	☐ Do Activity 8, p. 38 as a writing activity. ☐ Do Activity 9, p. 38 as a writing activity. ☐ For additional practice, do Activity 1, p. 9 in the **Travaux Pratiques de Grammaire.** ☐ For additional practice, do Activities 2–3, pp. 14–15 in the **Cahier d'activités.** ☐ For additional practice, do Activity 2, CD 1 in the **Interactive CD–ROM Tutor.**
Study the **Vocabulaire** on page 39.	☐ Do Activity 12, p. 39 as a writing activity. Write what each person is doing. ☐ Do Activity 14, p. 40 as a writing activity. ☐ For additional practice, do Activities 2–3 p. 10 in the **Travaux Pratiques de Grammaire.** ☐ For additional practice, do Activity 4, p. 15 in the **Cahier d'activités.** ☐ For additional practice, do Activity 1, CD 1 in the **Interactive CD–ROM Tutor.**
Study the grammar presentation in the **Grammaire** box on page 39: the verb **conduire.**	☐ Do Activity 13, p. 40 as a writing activity. ☐ For additional practice, do Activity 2, p. 54 in the **Grammaire supplémentaire.** ☐ For additional practice, do Activity 4, p. 11 in the **Travaux Pratiques de Grammaire.** ☐ For additional practice, do Activity 6, p. 16 in the **Cahier d'activités.**

CHAPITRE 2

■ PREMIERE ETAPE Student Make-Up Assignments Checklist

Pupil's Edition, pp. 40–41

Study the expressions in the **Comment dit–on...?** box on page 40: expressing impatience; reassuring someone. You should know how to express impatience and how to reassure someone.	☐ Do Activity 17, p. 41 as a writing activity. ☐ Do Activity 7, p. 16 in the **Cahier d'activités**.
Study the grammar presentation in the **Grammaire** box on page 41: the imperative.	☐ Do Activity 18, p. 41. ☐ For additional practice, do Activities 3–6, pp. 54–55 in the **Grammaire supplémentaire**. ☐ For additional practice, do Activities 5–7, pp. 11–12 in the **Travaux pratiques de grammaire**. ☐ For additional practice, do Activity 9, p. 17 in the **Cahier d'activités**. ☐ For additional practice, do Activity 3, CD 1 in the **Interactive CD–ROM Tutor**.

■ PREMIERE ETAPE Self-Test

Can you ask for and give directions?	How would you ask someone for directions to Brussels? How would you give someone directions from your home to... 1. your school? 2. your best friend's house? 3. the nearest grocery store?
Can you express impatience?	How would you express impatience if... 1. you wanted to leave, but your friend wouldn't get ready? 2. your friend wanted to stop and look in a music store on the way to the movies? 3. you were hurrying to class with a friend who suddenly stopped to talk to someone?
Can you reassure someone?	For each of the three situations above, what would the person say to reassure you?

CHAPITRE 2

For an online self-test, go to **go.hrw.com**.

WA3 FRANCOPHONE EUROPE–2

CHAPITRE 2

Belgique, nous voilà!

■ DEUXIEME ETAPE Student Make-Up Assignments Checklist

Pupil's Edition, p. 45

Study the expressions in the **Comment dit-on...?** box on page 45: expressing enthusiasm and boredom. You should know how to express enthusiasm or boredom.	☐ Do Activity 12, p. 19 in the **Cahier d'activités**.
Study the **Vocabulaire** on page 45.	☐ Do Activity 26, p. 45 as a writing activity. ☐ For additional practice, do Activities 8–9, pp. 13-14 in the **Travaux Pratiques de Grammaire**. ☐ For additional practice, do Activity 13, p. 19 in the **Cahier d'activités**. ☐ For additional practice, do Activity 4, CD 1 in the **Interactive CD-ROM Tutor**.

Holt French 3 Allez, viens!, Chapter 2

■ DEUXIEME ETAPE Student Make-Up Assignments Checklist

Pupil's Edition, pp. 46–47

Study the grammar presentation in the **Grammaire** box on page 47: pronouns and their placement.	☐ Do Activity 27, p. 46. ☐ For additional practice, do Activities 7-11, pp. 55-57 in **Grammaire supplémentaire**. ☐ For additional practice, do Activities 10–15, pp. 14-17 in the **Travaux Pratiques de Grammaire**. ☐ For additional practice, do Activities 15-16, pp. 20-21 in the **Cahier d'activités**. ☐ For additional practice, do Activity 5, CD 1 in the **Interactive CD-ROM Tutor**.
Study the expressions in the **Comment dit-on...?** box on page 47: asking and telling where things are. You should know how to ask where something is and how to respond to the same questions.	☐ Do Activity 29, p. 47 as a writing activity. Write the conversation in a logical order. ☐ For additional practice, do Activity 18, p. 22 in the **Cahier d'activités**. ☐ For additional practice, do Activity 6, CD 1 in the **Interactive CD-ROM Tutor**.

CHAPITRE 2

■ DEUXIEME ETAPE Self-Test

Can you express enthusiasm and boredom?	How would you express your enthusiasm for three of your favorite TV shows and comic strips to a friend?
	How would you express your boredom with…
	1. playing golf?
	2. doing homework?
	3. watching a documentary?
	4. cleaning the house?
	5. listening to a lecture?
Can you ask and tell where things are?	What question would you ask to find…
	1. a telephone?
	2. the bathroom?
	3. the elevator?
	How would you tell a new student at your school to find…
	1. the bathroom?
	2. the cafeteria?
	3. the science lab?
	4. the principal's office?

CHAPITRE 2

 For an online self-test, go to **go.hrw.com**.

WA3 FRANCOPHONE EUROPE-2

CHAPITRE 3

Soyons responsables!

■ PREMIERE ETAPE Student Make-Up Assignments Checklist

Pupil's Edition, pp. 67–68

Study the **Vocabulaire** on page 67.	☐ Do Activity 7, p. 68 as a writing activity. Write which chores each person must do.
	☐ For additional practice, do Activities 1–4, pp. 18–19 in the **Travaux Pratiques de Grammaire**.
	☐ For additional practice, do Activities 2–3, p. 26 in the **Cahier d'activités**.
	☐ For additional practice, do Activity 1, CD 1 in the **Interactive CD–ROM Tutor**.
Study the expressions in the **Comment dit–on...?** box on page 68: asking for, granting, and refusing permission; expressing obligation. You should know how to ask, grant and refuse permission, and to express obligation. You should also review the verb **devoir**.	☐ Do Activities 1–2, p. 84 in the **Grammaire supplémentaire**.
	☐ For additional practice, do Activities 5–6 p. 20 in the **Travaux Pratiques de Grammaire**.
	☐ For additional practice, do Activity 5, p. 27 in the **Cahier d'activités**.
	☐ For additional practice, do Activities 2–3, CD 1 in the **Interactive CD–ROM Tutor**.

CHAPITRE 3

■ PREMIERE ETAPE Student Make-Up Assignments Checklist

Pupil's Edition, pp. 69–71

Study the expressions in the **Grammaire** box on page 69: the subjuntive.	☐ Do Activity 10, p. 69. Complete the sentences in the picture with the expressions in the box.
	☐ Do Activity 11, p. 70.
	☐ For additional practice, do Activities 3–6, pp. 85–86 in the **Grammaire supplémentaire.**
	☐ For additional practice, do Activities 7–15, pp. 21–25 in the **Travaux pratiques de grammaire.**
	☐ For additional practice, do Activities 7–8, p. 28 in the **Cahier d'activités.**
	☐ For additional practice, do Activity 4, CD 1 in the **Interactive CD–ROM Tutor.**
Study the **Vocabulaire** on page 70.	☐ Do Activity 14, p. 71 as a writing activity.
	☐ Do Activity 16, p. 71 as a writing activity.
	☐ For additional practice, do Activities 16–17, p. 26 in the **Travaux pratiques de grammaire.**
	☐ For additional practice, do Activity 9, p. 29 in the **Cahier d'activités.**

■ PREMIERE ETAPE Self-Test

Can you ask for, grant, and refuse permission?	How would you ask permission to do something with a friend? If you were a parent, how would you give your teenager permission to do something? How would you refuse permission? What would you say to a friend who wanted to borrow your favorite cassette or CD?
Can you express obligation?	How would you tell your brother or sister that he or she has to… 1. do the laundry? 2. take out the dog? 3. mow the lawn?

 For an online self-test, go to **go.hrw.com**.

WA3 FRANCOPHONE EUROPE–3

CHAPITRE 3

Soyons responsables!

■ DEUXIEME ETAPE Student Make-Up Assignments Checklist

Pupil's Edition, p. 75

Study the expressions in the **Comment dit–on...?** box on page 75: forbidding. You should know how forbid certain activities.	☐ Do Activity 24, p. 75 as a writing activity. Match the signs with the forbidden activity. ☐ For additional practice, do Activity 22, p. 28 in the **Travaux Pratiques de Grammaire.**
Study the expressions in the **Note de Grammaire** box on page 75: negative with infinitives. You should know how to use negation with infinitives.	☐ Do Activities 7–9, pp. 86–87 in the **Grammaire supplémentaire.** ☐ For additional practice, do Activities 18–19, p. 27 in the **Travaux Pratiques de Grammaire.** ☐ For additional practice, do Activity 5, CD 1 in the **Interactive CD–ROM Tutor.**

CHAPITRE 3

■ DEUXIEME ETAPE Student Make-Up Assignments Checklist

Pupil's Edition, pp. 77–78

Study the **Vocabulaire** on page 77.	☐ Do Activity 28, p. 77 as a writing activity. ☐ For additional practice, do Activities 20–22, p. 28 in the **Travaux Pratiques de Grammaire.** ☐ For additional practice, do Activity 14, p. 31 in the **Cahier d'activités.** ☐ For additional practice, do Activity 6, CD 1 in the **Interactive CD–ROM Tutor.**
Study the expressions in the **Comment dit–on...?** box on page 78: reproaching; justifying your actions; rejecting others' excuses. You should know how to reproach someone, justify your actions, and reject someone's excuse.	☐ Do Activity 30, p. 78 as a writing activity. ☐ Do Activity 31, p. 78 as a writing activity. ☐ For additional practice, do Activities 16–18, pp. 32–33 in the **Cahier d'activités.**

CHAPITRE 3

■ DEUXIEME ETAPE Self-Test

Can you forbid someone to do something?	How would you forbid someone to… 1. smoke ? 2. park? 3. eat and drink?
Can you reproach someone?	What can you say to someone who… 1. throws trash out the car window? 2. uses aerosol sprays around the house? 3. smokes? How would you reproach someone who… 1. plays music too loud? 2. leaves all the lights on in the house?
Can you justify your actions and reject others' excuses?	What would you say to justify an action of yours that angered someone? What would you say to a child who makes excuses for doing something wrong?

 For an online self-test, go to **go.hrw.com**.

WA3 FRANCOPHONE EUROPE–3

CHAPITRE 3

CHAPITRE

4 Des goûts et des couleurs

■ PREMIERE ETAPE Student Make-Up Assignments Checklist

Pupil's Edition, pp. 97–99

Study the **Vocabulaire** on page 97.	☐ Do Activity 8, p. 98 as a writing activity. ☐ For additional practice, do Activities 1–7, pp. 29–32 in the **Travaux Pratiques de Grammaire.** ☐ For additional practice, do Activities 2–3, p. 38 in the **Cahier d'activités.** ☐ For additional practice, do Activity 1, CD 1 in the **Interactive CD–ROM Tutor**
Study the expressions in the **Comment dit–on...?** box on page 98: asking for and giving opinions. You should know how to ask for an opinion. You should also know how to give a favorable or an unfavorable opinion.	☐ Do Activity 11, p. 99 as a writing activity. Write the possible conversations. ☐ For additional practice, do Activity 4, p. 38 in the **Cahier d'activités.** ☐ For additional practice, do Activity 2, CD 1 in the **Interactive CD–ROM Tutor.**
Study the **Vocabulaire** box on page 99.	☐ Do Activity 12, p. 99 as a writing activity. Write your opinion of the different outfits your friends are wearing. ☐ For additional practice, do Activities 8–12, pp. 32–34 in the **Travaux Pratiques de Grammaire.** ☐ For additional practice, do Activity 5, p. 39 in the **Cahier d'activités.**

CHAPITRE 4

■ PREMIERE ETAPE Student Make-Up Assignments Checklist

Pupil's Edition, pp. 100–102

Study the expressions in the **Comment dit–on...?** box on page 100: asking which one(s); pointing out and identifying people and things. You should know how to ask which one(s) someone is talking about. You should also know how to point out and identify people and things.	☐ For additional practice, do Activity 7, p. 40 in the **Cahier d'activités.**
Study the grammar presentation in the **Grammaire** box on page 101: the interrogative and demonstrative pronouns.	☐ Do Activity 18, p. 101. ☐ Do Activity 19, p. 102 as a writing activity. ☐ Do Activity 20, p. 102. ☐ For additional practice, do Activities 1–3, pp. 114–115 in the **Grammaire supplémentaire.** ☐ For additional practice, do Activities 13–17, pp. 35–37 in the **Travaux pratiques de grammaire.** ☐ For additional practice, do Activity 8, p. 40 in the **Cahier d'activités.** ☐ For additional practice, do Activity 3, CD 1 in the **Interactive CD–ROM Tutor.**

Holt French 3 Allez, viens!, Chapter 4

■ PREMIERE ETAPE Self-Test

Can you ask for and give opinions?	How would you ask your friend's opinion of... 1. a green and white stripes polo shirt? 2. black leather pants? 3. a plaid mini–skirt? How would you give your opinion of these same items if you liked them? If you disliked them?
Can you ask which one(s)?	Your friend is pointing out some things she likes, but you can't tell which one(s) she's talking about. How do you ask if it's... 1. a purse? 2. a skirt? 3. gloves?
Can you point out and identify people and things?	How would your friend answer your questions above? How would you identify the following people if you didn't know their names? 1. a young man wearing a hat 2. a girl wearing glasses

For an online self-test, go to **go.hrw.com**.

WA3 FRANCOPHONE EUROPE–4

Nom_____ Classe_____ Date_____

4 Des goûts et des couleurs

■ DEUXIEME ETAPE Student Make-Up Assignments Checklist
Pupil's Edition, pp. 106–107

Study the **Vocabulaire** on page 106.	☐ Do Activity 27, p. 106 as a writing activity. Write a conversation between you and a friend.
	☐ For additional practice, do Activities 18–21, pp. 38–39 in the **Travaux pratiques de grammaire**.
	☐ For additional practice, do Activities 12–15, pp. 43–44 in the **Cahier d'activités**.
	☐ For additional practice, do Activity 4, CD 1 in the **Interactive CD–ROM Tutor**.
Study the expressions in the **Note de Grammaire** box on page 107: the causative **faire**.	☐ Do Activity 28, p. 107 as a writing activity.
	☐ Do Activity 29, p. 107 as a writing activity. Write a conversation where you give her some advice.
	☐ Do Activities 4, 6–7, pp. 116–117 in the **Grammaire supplémentaire**.
	☐ For additional practice, do Activities 22–23, p. 40 in the **Travaux pratiques de grammaire**.
	☐ For additional practice, do Activity 16, p. 45 in the **Cahier d'activités**.
	☐ For additional practice, do Activity 5, CD 1 in the **Interactive CD–ROM Tutor**.

■ DEUXIEME ETAPE Student Make-Up Assignments Checklist

Pupil's Edition, pp. 108–109

Study the expressions in the **Comment dit–on...?** box on page 108: paying and responding to compliments; reassuring someone. You should know how to pay a compliment and how to respond to one. You should also know how to reassure someone.

☐ Do Activity 32, p. 109 as a writing activity.

☐ Do Activity 33, p. 109 as a writing activity.

☐ Do Activity 5, p. 116 in the **Grammaire supplémentaire.**

☐ For additional practice, do Activities 17–20, pp. 45–46 in the **Cahier d'activités.**

☐ For additional practice, do Activity 6, CD 1 in the **Interactive CD–ROM Tutor.**

CHAPITRE 4

■ DEUXIEME ETAPE Self-Test

Can you pay and respond to a compliment?	How would you compliment a friend on an article of clothing?
	How would you respond if someone complimented you on your clothing?
Can you reassure someone?	What would you say to reassure a friend who is uncertain about a new haircut or article of clothing?

 For an online self-test, go to **go.hrw.com**.

WA3 FRANCOPHONE EUROPE–4

CHAPITRE 5

C'est notre avenir

■ PREMIÈRE ÉTAPE Student Make-Up Assignments Checklist

Pupil's Edition, pp. 132–133

Study the **Vocabulaire** on page 132.	☐ Do Activity 3, p. 50 in the **Cahier d'activités.** ☐ For additional practice, do Activities 1–4, pp. 41–42 in the **Travaux Pratiques de Grammaire.** ☐ For additional practice, do Activity 1, CD 2 in the **Interactive CD–ROM Tutor.**
Study the expressions in the **Comment dit–on…?** box on page 133: asking about and expressing intentions; expressing conditions and possibilities. You should know how to ask about intentions and how to express intentions, conditions and possibilities.	☐ Do Activity 8, p. 133 as a writing activity. Write what Bertille is thinking according to the pictures. ☐ For additional practice, do Activities 5–7, pp. 43–44 in the **Travaux Pratiques de Grammaire.** ☐ For additional practice, do Activities 4–6, pp. 50–51 in the **Cahier d'activités.**

CHAPITRE 5

■ PREMIERE ETAPE Student Make-Up Assignments Checklist

Pupil's Edition, pp. 134–135

Study the grammar presentation in the **Grammaire** box on page 134: the future	☐ Do Activity 9, p. 134. Conjugate the verbs in the correct form of the future.
	☐ Do Activity 10, p. 135 as a writing activity. Write a paragraph about Safiétou's and Penda's future.
	☐ Do Activity 11, p. 135 as a writing activity. Using the future tense, write what Adjoua will do according to the pictures.
	☐ For additional practice, do Activities 2–4, pp. 148–149 in the **Grammaire supplémentaire.**
	☐ For additional practice, do Activities 8–13, pp. 45–48 in the **Travaux pratiques de grammaire.**
	☐ For additional practice, do Activities 8–9, p. 52 in the **Cahier d'activités.**
	☐ For additional practice, do Activity 2, CD 2 in the **Interactive CD–ROM Tutor.**

CHAPITRE 5

■ PREMIERE ETAPE Self-Test

Can you ask about and express intentions?	How would you ask a friend what he or she plans to do after graduation?
	How would you tell what you plan to do in the future?
Can you express conditions and possibilities?	How would you tell someone what you will do, given these conditions?
	1. Si je me marie, …
	2. Si je vais à l'université, …
	3. Si je gagne de l'argent, …
	4. Si je trouve un travail, …
	How would you tell someone that you might do these things?
	1. look for a job
	2. get married
	3. go camping

For an online self-test, go to **go.hrw.com**.

WA3 FRANCOPHONE AFRICA–5

CHAPITRE 5

C'est notre avenir

■ **DEUXIEME ETAPE** Student Make-Up Assignments Checklist

Pupil's Edition, pp. 139–141

Study the **Vocabulaire** on page 139.	☐ Do Activity 19, p. 140 as a writing activity.
	☐ For additional practice, do Activities 14–17, pp. 49–50 in the **Travaux Pratiques de Grammaire.**
	☐ For additional practice, do Activities 13–14, p. 55 in the **Cahier d'activités.**
	☐ For additional practice, do Activity 3, CD 2 in the **Interactive CD–ROM Tutor.**
Study the expressions in the **Comment dit–on...?** box on page 140: asking about future plans; expressing wishes; expressing indecision; giving advice. You should know how to ask about future plans; how to express wishes and indecision; and how to give advice.	☐ Do Activity 23, p. 141 as a writing activity. Write a conversation between you and a friend.
	☐ For additional practice, do Activities 15–16, pp. 55–56 in the **Cahier d'activités.**
	☐ For additional practice, do Activity 4, CD 2 in the **Interactive CD–ROM Tutor.**

CHAPITRE 5

Holt French 3 Allez, viens!, Chapter 5

Nom_____ Classe_____ Date_____

■ DEUXIEME ETAPE Student Make-Up Assignments Checklist
Pupil's Edition, pp. 141–143

Study the expressions in the **Grammaire** box on page 141: the conditional.	☐ Do Activity 24, p. 142 as a writing activity. ☐ For additional practice, do Activities 5–7, pp. 150–151 in the **Grammaire supplémentaire**. ☐ For additional practice, do Activities 18–20, pp. 51–52 in the **Travaux Pratiques de Grammaire**. ☐ For additional practice, do Activities 17–19, pp. 56–57 in the **Cahier d'activités**. ☐ For additional practice, do Activity 5, CD 2 in the **Interactive CD–ROM Tutor**.
Study the expressions in the **Comment dit–on...?** box on page 142: requesting information; writing a formal letter. You should know how to ask for information and how to write a letter.	☐ Do Activity 21, p. 58 in the **Cahier d'activités**. ☐ For additional practice, do Activity 6, CD 2 in the **Interactive CD–ROM Tutor**.
Study the expressions in the **Note de Grammaire** box on page 143: **inversion**.	☐ Do Activity 27, p. 143. ☐ Do Activity 28, p. 143 as a writing activity. ☐ For additional practice, do Activities 8–9, p. 151 in the **Grammaire supplémentaire**. ☐ For additional practice, do Activity 21, p. 53 in the **Travaux Pratiques de Grammaire**.

CHAPITRE 5

■ DEUXIEME ETAPE Self-Test

Can you ask about future plans?	What would you ask someone about his or her future plans?
Can you express wishes?	How would you tell what you would like to do in the future?
Can you express indecision?	How would you express indecision about your future?
Can you give advice?	How would you advise a friend who... 1. failed an exam? 2. doesn't have any pocket money? 3. would like to go to college? 4. wants to be a teacher? 5. is uncertain about his or her choice of profession?
Can you request information and write a formal letter?	How would you request information about courses, costs, and so forth from a school or a university? How would you write the closing of the letter you just wrote?

 For an online self-test, go to **go.hrw.com**.

WA3 FRANCOPHONE AFRICA–5

CHAPITRE 6

Ma famille, mes copains et moi

■ PREMIERE ETAPE Student Make-Up Assignments Checklist

Pupil's Edition, pp. 161–163

Study the expressions in the **Comment dit–on...?** box on page 161: making, accepting, and refusing suggestions. You should know how to make a suggestion and how to either accept or refuse a suggestion.	☐ Do Activity 8, p. 161 as a writing activity. ☐ Do Activity 2, p. 62 in the **Cahier d'activités.** ☐ For additional practice, do Activity 2, CD 2 in the **Interactive CD–ROM Tutor.**
Study the expressions in the **Comment dit–on...?** box on page 162: making arrangements. You should know how to make arrangements with friends.	☐ For additional practice, do Activity 4, p. 62 in the **Cahier d'activités.** ☐ For additional practice, do Activity 2, CD 2 in the **Interactive CD–ROM Tutor.**
Study the expressions in the **Grammaire** box on page 162: reciprocal verbs.	☐ Do Activity 11, p. 162. ☐ Do Activity 12, p. 163 as a writing activity. ☐ Do Activity 13, p. 163. ☐ For additional practice, do Activities 1–2, p. 178 in the **Grammaire supplémentaire.** ☐ For additional practice, do Activities 1–7, pp. 54–57 in the **Travaux pratiques de grammaire.** ☐ For additional practice, do Activities 5–6, p. 63 in the **Cahier d'activités.** ☐ For additional practice, do Activity 1, CD 2 in the **Interactive CD–ROM Tutor.**

CHAPITRE 6

■ PREMIERE ETAPE Student Make-Up Assignments Checklist

Pupil's Edition, p. 164

Study the expressions in the **Comment dit–on...?** box on page 164: making and accepting apologies. You should know how to apologize and how to accept someone's apology.	☐ For additional practice, do Activity 8, p. 64 in the **Cahier d'activités**. ☐ For additional practice, do Activity 2, CD 2 in the **Interactive CD–ROM Tutor**.
Study the grammar presentation in the **Grammaire** box on page 164: the past infinitive	☐ Do Activity 16, p. 164 as a writing activity. Write how Aïcha will apologize for her misbehaviors listed. ☐ For additional practice, do Activity 3, p. 179 in the **Grammaire supplémentaire**. ☐ For additional practice, do Activities 8–11, pp. 58–59 in the **Travaux pratiques de grammaire**. ☐ For additional practice, do Activity 9, p. 65 in the **Cahier d'activités**. ☐ For additional practice, do Activity 3, CD 2 in the **Interactive CD–ROM Tutor**.

CHAPITRE 6

Holt French 3 Allez, viens!, Chapter 6

■ PREMIERE ETAPE Self-Test

Can you make, accept, and refuse suggestions?	How would you suggest to a friend to... 1. go dancing? 2. play tennis? 3. watch movies on TV? How would you accept these suggestions? How would you refuse these suggestions?
Can you make arrangements?	You and a friend have decided to do one of the activities listed above. What would you say to make the necessary arrangements?
Can you make and accept apologies?	You've just broken your best friend's CD player. How do you apologize?

 For an online self-test, go to **go.hrw.com**.

WA3 FRANCOPHONE AFRICA–6

CHAPITRE 6

CHAPITRE **6**

Ma famille, mes copains et moi

■ **DEUXIEME ETAPE** Student Make-Up Assignments Checklist

Pupil's Edition, pp. 169–172

Study the expressions in the **Comment dit–on...?** box on page 169: showing and responding to hospitality; expressing and responding to thanks. You should know how to show hospitality to a guest. You should also know how to thank someone for their hospitality.	☐ Do Activity 25, p. 170 as a writing activity. Match each thank you with the appropriate response.
	☐ Do Activity 26, p. 170 as a writing activity.
	☐ For additional practice, do Activity 4, p. 179 in the **Grammaire supplémentaire**.
	☐ For additional practice, do Activity 12, p. 67 in the **Cahier d'activités**.
	☐ For additional practice, do Activity 4, CD 2 in the **Interactive CD–ROM Tutor**.
Study the **Vocabulaire** on page 171.	☐ Do Activity 29, p. 172.
	☐ Do Activity 31, p. 172.
	☐ For additional practice, do Activities 12–17, pp. 60–62 in the **Travaux pratiques de grammaire**.
	☐ For additional practice, do Activities 13–14, pp. 68–69 in the **Cahier d'activités**.
	☐ For additional practice, do Activity 5, CD 2 in the **Interactive CD–ROM Tutor**.

CHAPITRE 6

■ DEUXIEME ETAPE Student Make-Up Assignments Checklist

Pupil's Edition, p. 173

Study the expressions in the **Comment dit–on...?** box on page 173: quarreling. You should know how to accuse someone and respond to an accusation. You should also know how to justify a quarrel.

☐ Do Activity 33, p. 173 as a writing activity. Write a dialogue where you tell your brother or sister they're bugging you and the quarrel that follows.

☐ For additional practice, do Activities 5–7, pp. 180–181 in the **Grammaire supplémentaire**.

☐ For additional practice, do Activities 15–17, p. 70 in the **Cahier d'activités**.

☐ For additional practice, do Activity 6, CD 2 in the **Interactive CD–ROM Tutor**.

CHAPITRE 6

DEUXIEME ETAPE Self-Test

Can you show and respond to hospitality?	What would you say to your guests when…
	1. they've just arrived at your home?
	2. you've taken their coats and they're standing inside the doorway?
	3. you'd like to offer them something to eat or drink?
	How would you respond as a guest in each of the situations above?
Can you express and respond to thanks?	How would you thank these people?
	1. A good friend lends you a new CD.
	2. A stranger stops to help pick up some things you've dropped.
	How would you respond if you were the people above?
Can you quarrel?	What would you say in the following situations?
	1. Your sister is annoying you while you try to do your homework.
	2. You get in trouble for something your classmate did.
	3. Your little brother enters your room and starts looking through your things.

For an online self-test, go to **go.hrw.com**.

WA3 FRANCOPHONE AFRICA–6

CHAPITRE 6

Nom_____ Classe_____ Date_____

7 Un safari-photo

■ PREMIERE ETAPE Student Make-Up Assignments Checklist

Pupil's Edition, pp. 192–193

Study the **Vocabulaire** on page 192.	☐ Do Activity 8, p. 192 as a writing activity.
	☐ For additional practice, do Activities 1–3, pp. 63–64 in the **Travaux pratiques de grammaire**.
	☐ For additional practice, do Activity 2, p. 74 in the **Cahier d'activités**.
	☐ For additional practice, do Activity 1, CD 2 in the **Interactive CD–ROM Tutor**.
Study the expressions in the **Comment dit–on...?** box on page 193: making suppositions; expressing doubt and certainty. You should know how to make suppositions and how to express doubt and certainty.	☐ For additional practice, do Activity 3, pp. 74–75 in the **Cahier d'activités**.
	☐ For additional practice, do Activity 3, CD 2 in the **Interactive CD–ROM Tutor**.
Study the expressions in the **Note de Grammaire** box on page 193: when to use the subjuntive.	☐ Do Activity 10, p. 193 as a writing activity. Write a conversation between you and a friend in which you discuss how a safari would be.
	☐ For additional practice, do Activity 4, pp. 64–65 in the **Travaux pratiques de grammaire**.

CHAPITRE 7

■ PREMIERE ETAPE Student Make-Up Assignments Checklist

Pupil's Edition, pp. 194–196

Study the **Vocabulaire** on page 194.	☐ Do Activity 12, p. 194 as a writing activity. Write her a note telling her what she has forgotten to pack.
	☐ For additional practice, do Activities 5–6, pp. 65–66 in the **Travaux pratiques de grammaire.**
	☐ For additional practice, do Activity 4, p. 75 in the **Cahier d'activités.**
	☐ For additional practice, do Activity 2, CD 2 in the **Interactive CD–ROM Tutor.**
Study the expressions in the **Comment dit–on...?** box on page 195: asking for and giving advice. You should know how to ask for advice, how to respond to advice, and how to give advice.	☐ Do Activity 14, p. 195.
	☐ For additional practice, do Activity 5, p. 75 in the **Cahier d'activités.**
	☐ For additional practice, do Activity 3, CD 2 in the **Interactive CD–ROM Tutor.**
Study the grammar presentation in the **Grammaire** box on page 196: using the subjunctive.	☐ Do Activity 15, p. 196 as a writing activity.
	☐ For additional practice, do Activities 2–4, pp. 208–209 in **Grammaire supplémentaire.**
	☐ For additional practice, do Activities 7–9, pp. 66–68 in the **Travaux pratiques de grammaire.**
	☐ For additional practice, do Activity 6, p. 76 in the **Cahier d'activités.**
	☐ For additional practice, do Activity 4, CD 2 in the **Interactive CD–ROM Tutor.**

■ PREMIERE ETAPE Self-Test

Can you make suppositions?	How would you make suppositions about what you would see on a safari?
Can you express doubt and certainty?	How would you express your doubt or certainty about seeing the following animals on safari in Africa? 1. a kangaroo 2. a zebra 3. a polar bear 4. a giraffe
Can you ask for and give advice?	How would you ask whether these items are necessary? 1. mosquito repellent 2. binoculars 3. traveler's checks How would you tell a friend whether the items above are necessary for… 1. a trip to Africa? 2. a trip to the North Pole?

 For an online self-test, go to **go.hrw.com**.

WA3 FRANCOPHONE AFRICA–7

Nom_____ Classe_____ Date_____

7 Un safari-photo

■ DEUXIEME ETAPE Student Make-Up Assignments Checklist

Pupil's Edition, pp. 200–201

Study the **Vocabulaire** on page 200.	☐ Do Activity 22, p. 200. ☐ Do Activity 24, p. 201 as a writing activity. ☐ For additional practice, do Activities 10–11, p. 69 in the **Travaux pratiques de grammaire.** ☐ For additional practice, do Activities 10–11, pp. 79–80 in the **Cahier d'activités.** ☐ For additional practice, do Activity 5, CD 2 in the **Interactive CD–ROM Tutor.**
Study the expressions in the **Comment dit–on...?** box on page 201: expressing astonishment. You should know how to express astonishment.	☐ Do Activity 26, p. 201. ☐ For additional practice, do Activity 12, p. 81 in the **Cahier d'activités.**

■ DEUXIEME ETAPE Student Make-Up Assignments Checklist

Pupil's Edition, pp. 202–203

Study the expressions in the **Comment dit–on...?** box on page 202: cautioning someone; expressing fear; reassuring someone; expressing relief. You should know how to caution or reassure someone, and how to express fear and relief.

☐ Do Activity 29 p. 202 as a writing activity.

☐ Do Activity 30 p. 202 as a writing activity. Write what would you say to warn the people in each illustration.

☐ For additional practice, do Activities 12–13, p. 70 in **Travaux pratiques de grammaire.**

☐ For additional pracatice, do Activity 13, p. 81 in the **Cahier d'activités.**

Study the grammar presentation in the **Grammaire** box on page 203: irregular subjuntive forms.

☐ Do Activity 31, p. 203.

☐ For additional practice, do Activities 5–8, pp. 210–211 in the **Grammaire supplémentaire.**

☐ For additional practice, do Activities 14–16, pp. 71–72 in the **Travaux pratiques de grammaire.**

☐ For additional practice, do Activity 14, p. 82 in the **Cahier d'activités.**

☐ For additional practice, do Activity 6, CD 2 in the **Interactive CD–ROM Tutor.**

CHAPITRE 7

■ DEUXIEME ETAPE Self-Test

Can you express astonishment?	How would you express your feelings about something really impressive?
Can you caution someone?	How would you warn people in these situations? 1. A friend is about to step out into a busy street without looking. 2. A relative is traveling to a country where mosquitoes carry malaria. 3. A friend is approached by a mean dog.
Can you express fear?	How would you express fear of... 1. snakes and spider? 2. a horror movie you're watching?
Can you reassure someone?	How would you reassure someone who is afraid of the things above?
Can you express relief?	How would you express your relief at... 1. not getting bitten by a mean dog? 2. not getting a bad grade at school?

 For an online self-test, go to **go.hrw.com**.

WA3 FRANCOPHONE AFRICA–7

Nom _____ Classe _____ Date _____

8 La Tunisie, pays de contrastes

■ PREMIÈRE ÉTAPE Student Make-Up Assignments Checklist

Pupil's Edition, pp. 222–224

Study the expressions in the **Comment dit–on...?** box on page 222: asking someone to convey good wishes; closing a letter. You should know how to ask someone to convey good wishes and how to close a letter.	☐ Do Activity 8, p. 222. ☐ For additional practice, do Activity 2, p. 86 in the **Cahier d'activités.** ☐ For additional practice, do Activity 1, CD 2 in the **Interactive CD–ROM Tutor.**
Study the **Vocabulaire** on page 223.	☐ Do Activity 13, p. 224 as a writing activity. Write what you see and the activities done in each region. ☐ For additional practice, do Activities 1–3, pp. 73–74 in the **Travaux pratiques de grammaire.** ☐ For additional practice, do Activities 3–5, pp. 86–87 in the **Cahier d'activités.** ☐ For additional practice, do Activity 2, CD 2 in the **Interactive CD–ROM Tutor.**

■ PREMIERE ETAPE Student Make-Up Assignments Checklist

Pupil's Edition, pp. 225–226

Study the expressions in the **Comment dit–on...?** box on page 225: expressing hopes or wishes; giving advice. You should know how to express hope and wishes, and how to give advice.	☐ Activities are combined with the **Grammaire** section below.
Study the grammar presentation in the **Grammaire** box on page 225: **si** clauses.	☐ Do Activity 15, p. 225 as a writing activity.
	☐ Do Activity 16, p. 226 as a writing activity. Write what each person would like to do.
	☐ Do Activity 17, p. 226 as a writing activity. Write a conversation between you and a friend.
	☐ For additional practice, do Activities 2–5, pp. 238–240 in the **Grammaire supplémentaire**.
	☐ For additional practice, do Activities 4–9, pp. 74–77 in the **Travaux pratiques de grammaire**.
	☐ For additional practice, do Activities 6–7, p. 88 in the **Cahier d'activités**.
	☐ For additional practice, do Activity 3, CD 2 in the **Interactive CD–ROM Tutor**.

CHAPITRE 8

■ PREMIERE ETAPE Self-Test

Can you ask someone to convey good wishes?	A friend who has been visiting you is about to go back home to his or her family. What would you say to send your best wishes?
Can you close a letter?	How would you end a letter to a friend?
Can you express hopes and wishes?	How would you express a wish to… 1. travel in Africa? 2. buy a new car? 3. go to college?
Can you give advice?	What advice would you give to a friend… 1. who's having trouble with a school subject? 2. whose parents are very strict? 3. who wants to live in another country?

For an online self-test, go to **go.hrw.com**.

WA3 FRANCOPHONE AFRICA–8

CHAPITRE 8

CHAPITRE 8

La Tunisie, pays de contrastes

■ DEUXIEME ETAPE Student Make-Up Assignments Checklist

Pupil's Edition, pp. 230–231

Study the **Vocabulaire** on page 230.	☐ Do Activity 26, p. 230.
	☐ For additional practice, do Activities 10–13, pp. 78–79 in the **Travaux pratiques de grammaire**.
	☐ For additional practice, do Activity 13, p. 91 in the **Cahier d'activités**.
	☐ For additional practice, do Activity 4, CD 2 in the **Interactive CD–ROM Tutor**.
Study the expressions in the **Comment dit–on...?** box on page 231: complaining; expressing annoyance. You should know how to complain and how to express annoyance at someone.	☐ Do Activity 29, p. 231.
	☐ For additional practice, do Activities 14–15, p. 92 in the **Cahier d'activités**.

CHAPITRE 8

■ DEUXIEME ETAPE Student Make-Up Assignments Checklist

Pupil's Edition, pp. 232–233

Study the expressions in the **Comment dit–on...?** box on page 232: making comparisons. You should know how to compare.	☐ Do Activity 31 p. 232 as a writing activity. Place statements into two columns; one for Latifa and the other for Mona. ☐ For additional pracatice, do Activity 16, p. 93 in the **Cahier d'activités.** ☐ For additional practice, do Activity 5, CD 2 in the **Interactive CD–ROM Tutor.**
Study the grammar presentation in the **Grammaire** box on page 232: the comparative.	☐ Do Activity 32, p. 233 as a writing activity. ☐ Do Activity 33, p. 233 as a writing activity. ☐ For additional practice, do Activities 6–9, pp. 240–241 in the **Grammaire supplémentaire.** ☐ For additional practice, do Activities 14–16, pp. 80–81 in the **Travaux pratiques de grammaire.** ☐ For additional practice, do Activities 17–18, pp. 93–94 in the **Cahier d'activités.** ☐ For additional practice, do Activity 6, CD 2 in the **Interactive CD–ROM Tutor.**

CHAPITRE 8

■ DEUXIEME ETAPE Self-Test

Can you complain?	What would you say to complain if...
	1. you missed the bus?
	2. your neighbor was mowing the lawn while you are trying to sleep?
	3. people were bumping into you on the street?
Can you express annoyance?	How would express you annoyance if...
	1. someone shoved in front of you as you were boarding the bus?
	2. someone grabbed an item from you that you wanted to buy?
	3. the people behind you at the movies were talking loudly during the film?
Can you make comparisons?	How would you compare the following?
	1. your favorite and least favorite school subjects
	2. the last two movies you saw
	3. two places you've lived or visited

 For an online self-test, go to **go.hrw.com**.

WA3 FRANCOPHONE AFRICA–8

CHAPITRE 8

CHAPITRE 9
C'est l'fun!

■ **PREMIERE ETAPE** Student Make-Up Assignments Checklist

Pupil's Edition, pp. 256–258

Study the **Vocabulaire** box on page 256.	☐ Do Activity 7, p. 256 as a writing activity.
	☐ For additional practice, do Activities 1–4, pp. 82–83 in **Travaux pratiques de grammaire.**
	☐ For additional practice, do Activity 2, p. 98 in the **Cahier d'activités.**
	☐ For additional practice, do Activity 1, CD 3 in the **Interactive CD–ROM Tutor.**
Study the expressions in the **Comment dit–on...?** box on page 257: agreeing and disagreeing; expressing indifference. You should know how to express agreement, disagreement and indifference.	☐ Do Activity 11, p. 257 as a writing activity. Write a conversation between you and a friend discussing the latest videos of the starts listed in the box. You should agree on some and disagree on some.
	☐ For additional practice, do Activity 4, p. 99 in the **Cahier d'activités.**
	☐ For additional practice, do Activity 3, CD 3 in the **Interactive CD–ROM Tutor.**
Study the **Vocabulaire** on page 226.	☐ Do Activity 13, p. 258 as a writing activity.
	☐ For additional practice, do Activities 5–6, p. 84 in **Travaux pratiques de grammaire.**
	☐ For additional practice, do Activities 5–6, pp. 99–100 in the **Cahier d'activités.**

CHAPITRE 9

■ PREMIERE ETAPE Student Make-Up Assignments Checklist

Pupil's Edition, pp. 258–260

Study the grammar presentation in the **Grammaire** box on page 258: negative expressions.	☐ Do Activity 14, p. 259 as a writing activity. ☐ For additional practice, do Activities 1–3, pp. 272–273 in the **Grammaire supplémentaire**. ☐ For additional practice, do Activities 7–9, pp. 85–86 in the **Travaux pratiques de grammaire**. ☐ For additional practice, do Activity 7, p. 100 in the **Cahier d'activités**. ☐ For additional practice, do Activity 2, CD 3 in the **Interactive CD–ROM Tutor**.
Study the grammar presentation in the **Note de Grammaire** box on page 259: **ne...que**.	☐ Do Activity 15, p. 259 as a writing activity. ☐ For additional practice, do Activity 4, p. 273 in the **Grammaire supplémentaire**. ☐ For additional practice, do Activity 10, p. 86 in the **Travaux pratiques de grammaire**.
Study the expressions in the **Comment dit–on...?** box on page 259: making requests. You should know how to ask someone to be quiet or adjust the volume.	☐ Do Activity 17, p. 260 as a writing activity. ☐ For additional practice, do Activity 9, p. 101 in the **Cahier d'activités**. ☐ For additional practice, do Activity 3, CD 3 in the **Interactive CD–ROM Tutor**.

CHAPITRE 9

Holt French 3 Allez, viens!, Chapter 9

■ PREMIERE ETAPE Self-Test

Can you agree and disagree?	You and a friend have just seen a movie together. Your friend thought the movie was great. How would you express your agreement with your friend?
	How would you say that you disagree with your friend's opinion of the movie?
Can you express indifference?	You friend wants to know which TV show you want to watch next. What do you say if you really have no opinion?
Can you make requests?	How would you ask the people in the following situations to be quiet?

	1. You're at movie and the people behind you are talking loudly.
	2. You're talking on the telephone and your brother has the TV turned up too loud.
	3. You're trying to watch a TV show and your little sister is making noise.

  For an online self-test, go to **go.hrw.com**.

WA3 FRANCOPHONE AMERICA–9

C H A P I T R E   9

9 C'est l'fun!

CHAPITRE

■ DEUXIEME ETAPE Student Make-Up Assignments Checklist

Pupil's Edition, pp. 264–265

Study the **Vocabulaire** on page 264.	☐ Do Activity 25, p. 264 as a writing activity. Write what kind of movie each phrase is describing.
	☐ Do Activity 26, p. 264 as a writing activity.
	☐ For additional practice, do Activity 11, p. 87 in the **Travaux pratiques de grammaire**.
	☐ For additional practice, do Activities 12–13, p. 103 in the **Cahier d'activités**.
	☐ For additional practice, do Activity 4, CD 3 in the **Interactive CD–ROM Tutor**.
Study the expressions in the **Comment dit–on…?** box on page 265: asking for and making judgments; asking for and making recommendations. You should know how to ask for a judgment or a recommendation. You should also know how to respond by giving either a positive or a negative judgment, or a recommendation.	☐ Do Activity 28, p. 265 as a writing activity.
	☐ For additional practice, do Activity 14, p. 104 in the **Cahier d'activités**.
	☐ For additional practice, do Activity 6, CD 3 in the **Interactive CD–ROM Tutor**.

CHAPITRE 9

■ DEUXIEME ETAPE Student Make-Up Assignments Checklist

Pupil's Edition, pp. 266–267

Study the expressions in the **Comment dit–on...?** box on page 266: asking about and summarizing a story. You should know how to ask about a story and how to summarize a story.	☐ For additional pracatice, do Activity 15, p. 105 in the **Cahier d'activités**. ☐ For additional practice, do Activity 6, CD 3 in the **Interactive CD–ROM Tutor**.
Study the grammar presentation in the **Grammaire** box on page 234: relative pronouns.	☐ Do Activity 31, p. 267. Match each sentence beginning to its correct ending. ☐ Do Activity 32, p. 267. Complete the paragraph with the correct relative pronoun. ☐ For additional practice, do Activities 5–9, pp. 273–275 in the **Grammaire supplémentaire**. ☐ For additional practice, do Activities 12–13, pp. 87–88 in the **Travaux pratiques de grammaire**. ☐ For additional practice, do Activities 16–17, pp. 105–106 in the **Cahier d'activités**. ☐ For additional practice, do Activity 5, CD 3 in the **Interactive CD–ROM Tutor**.

CHAPITRE 9

■ DEUXIEME ETAPE Self-Test

Can you ask for and make judgments?	How would you ask a friend her opinion of a TV program you've just seen together?
	How would you answer the question above if you liked the program? If you disliked the program?
Can you ask for and make recommendations?	How would you ask a friend if he or she recommends a movie?
	How would you recommend a movie you've just seen to a friend?
	What would you say if your friend wanted to go see a movie you thought was terrible?
Can you ask about and summarize a story?	How would you ask a friend what a movie was about?
	How would you tell someone about the last movie you saw?

 For an online self-test, go to **go.hrw.com**.

WA3 FRANCOPHONE AMERICA–9

10 Rencontres au soleil

■ **PREMIERE ETAPE** Student Make-Up Assignments Checklist

Pupil's Edition, pp. 286–288

Study the **Vocabulaire** on page 286.	☐ Do Activity 9, p. 287. ☐ For additional practice, do Activities 1–2, p. 89 in **Travaux pratiques de grammaire**. ☐ For additional practice, do Activities 2–3, p. 110 in the **Cahier d'activités**. ☐ For additional practice, do Activity 1, CD 3 in the **Interactive CD–ROM Tutor**.
Study the expressions in the **Comment dit–on…?** box on page 287: bragging; flattering. You should know how to brag and how to flatter someone.	☐ Do Activity 12, p. 288. ☐ For additional practice, do Activities 4–5, p. 111 in the **Cahier d'activités**. ☐ For additional practice, do Activity 3, CD 3 in the **Interactive CD–ROM Tutor**.

CHAPITRE 10

■ PREMIERE ETAPE Student Make-Up Assignments Checklist

Pupil's Edition, pp. 288–289

Study the grammar presentation in the **Grammaire** box on page 288: the superlative.	☐ Do Activity 13, p. 289. ☐ Do Activity 14, p. 289 as a writing activity. ☐ Do Activity 15, p. 289 as a writing activity. ☐ For additional practice, do Activities 1–4, pp. 302–303 in **Grammaire supplémentaire.** ☐ For additional practice, do Activities 3–7, pp. 90–92 in the **Travaux pratiques de grammaire.** ☐ For additional practice, do Activities 6–7, pp. 111–112 in the **Cahier d'activités.** ☐ For additional practice, do Activity 2, CD 3 in the **Interactive CD–ROM Tutor.**
Study the expressions in the **Comment dit–on...?** box on page 290: teasing. You should know how to tease someone and how to respond to teasing.	☐ Do Activity 18, p. 290 as a writing activity. ☐ For additional practice, do Activities 9–10, p. 113 in the **Cahier d'activités.** ☐ For additional practice, do Activity 3, CD 3 in the **Interactive CD–ROM Tutor.**

■ PREMIERE ETAPE Self-Test

Can you brag?	What would you say to brag in the following situations? 1. You finish an assignment before everyone else. 2. You win a race. 3. You get the highest grade on a test.
Can you flatter?	What would you say to flatter a person if he or she were… 1. really athletic? 2. a good student? 3. very artistic?
Can you tease?	What would you say to tease the people in these situations? 1. Your friend seems to have a crush on someone. 2. Your brother gets dressed to go out on a date and none of his clothes match. 3. You're playing tennis with a friend who keeps missing the ball. How would you respond to the teasing above.

 For an online self-test, go to **go.hrw.com**.

WA3 FRANCOPHONE AMERICA–10

10 Rencontres au soleil

■ DEUXIEME ETAPE Student Make-Up Assignments Checklist

Pupil's Edition, pp. 294–295

Study the **Vocabulaire** on page 294.	☐ Do Activity 27, p. 294.
	☐ For additional practice, do Activities 8–9, p. 93 in the **Travaux pratiques de grammaire.**
	☐ For additional practice, do Activities 12–13, p. 115 in the **Cahier d'activités.**
	☐ For additional practice, do Activity 4, CD 3 in the **Interactive CD–ROM Tutor.**
Study the expressions in the **Comment dit–on...?** box on page 295: breaking some news; showing interest; expressing disbelief. You should know how to break some news, how to show interest, and how to express disbelief.	☐ Do Activity 29, p. 295 as a writing activity. Write a conversation where you announce three unbelievable events using the expression in the box. Your friend expresses disbelief.
	☐ For additional practice, do Activity 14, p. 116 in the **Cahier d'activités.**
	☐ For additional practice, do Activity 5, CD 3 in the **Interactive CD–ROM Tutor.**

■ **DEUXIEME ETAPE** Student Make-Up Assignments Checklist

Pupil's Edition, pp. 295–297

Study the grammar presentation in the **Grammaire** box on page 295: the past perfect.	☐ Do Activity 30, p. 296.
	☐ Do Activity 31, p. 296 as a writing activity. Write a dialogue between you and your friend.
	☐ Do Activity 32, p. 296.
	☐ For additional practice, do Activities 5–6, pp. 304–305 in the **Grammaire supplémentaire.**
	☐ For additional practice, do Activities 10–12, pp. 94–95 in the **Travaux pratiques de grammaire.**
	☐ For additional practice, do Activities 16–17, p. 117 in the **Cahier d'activités.**
	☐ For additional practice, do Activity 6, CD 3 in the **Interactive CD–ROM Tutor.**
Study the expressions in the **Comment dit–on...?** box on page 297: telling a joke. You should know how to bring up, relate, and respond to a joke, and how to continue a story.	☐ Do Activity 35, p. 297 as a writing activity.
	☐ For additional practice, do Activity 7, p. 305 in the **Grammaire supplémentaire.**
	☐ For additional pracatice, do Activity 19, p. 118 in the **Cahier d'activités.**

Holt French 3 Allez, viens!, Chapter 10

■ DEUXIEME ETAPE Self-Test

Can you break some news?	How would you tell a friend what happened to the following people? 1. Jean gave Martine a diamond ring. 2. The Dupont moved. 3. Pierre fell and broke both legs.
Can you show interest?	How would you show interest in something a friend was saying?
Can you express disbelief?	What would you say if you didn't believe what your friend was telling you?
Can you tell a joke?	How would you introduce a joke? What would you say if you heard a joke you liked? What would you say if the joke were bad?

 For an online self-test, go to **go.hrw.com**.

WA3 FRANCOPHONE AMERICA–10

11 Laissez les bons temps rouler!

■ **PREMIERE ETAPE** Student Make-Up Assignments Checklist

Pupil's Edition, pp. 316–318

Study the expressions in the **Comment dit–on...?** box on page 316: asking for confirmation. You should know how to ask for confirmation.	☐ Do Activity 7, p. 316.
	☐ For additional practice, do Activities 2–3, p. 332 in the **Grammaire supplémentaire**.
	☐ For additional practice, do Activities 2–3, p. 122 in the **Cahier d'activités**.

Study the **Vocabulaire** on page 317.	☐ Do Activity 10, p. 317.
	☐ Do Activity 11, p. 318 as a writing activity.
	☐ For additional practice, do Activities 1–4, pp. 96–97 in **Travaux pratiques de grammaire**.
	☐ For additional practice, do Activities 4–5, p. 123 in the **Cahier d'activités**.
	☐ For additional practice, do Activity 1, CD 3 in the **Interactive CD–ROM Tutor**.

■ PREMIERE ETAPE Student Make-Up Assignments Checklist

Pupil's Edition, pp. 318–319

Study the expressions in the **Comment dit–on...?** box on page 318: asking for and giving opinions; agreeing and disagreeing. You should know how to ask for an opinion, how to give a positive or a negative opinion, and how to agree or disagree with someone's opinion.

☐ Do Activity 14, p. 319 as a writing activity.

☐ For additional practice, do Activities 6–8, pp. 124–125 in the **Cahier d'activités.**

☐ For additional practice, do Activity 2, CD 3 in the **Interactive CD–ROM Tutor.**

Holt French 3 Allez, viens!, Chapter 11

■ PREMIERE ETAPE Self-Test

Can you ask for confirmation?	You run into someone you haven't seen in a long time. Who would you ask for confirmation about... 1. his or her brother's name? 2. where he or she lives? 3. his or her age? 4. where he or she goes to school?
Can you ask for and give an opinion?	How would you ask a friend's opinion of your favorite music? How would you express your opinions about the following types of music? 1. le rock 2. le jazz 3. la musique classique 4. le country 5. le rap
Can you agree or disagree?	A friend gives you an opinion about a CD you've just bought. How would you express your agreement? What would you say if you don't agree with your friend?

CHAPITRE 11

For an online self-test, go to **go.hrw.com**.

WA3 FRANCOPHONE AMERICA–11

11 Laissez les bons temps rouler!

■ DEUXIEME ETAPE Student Make-Up Assignments Checklist

Pupil's Edition, pp. 323–325

Study the expressions in the **Comment dit–on…?** box on page 323: asking for explanations. You should know how to ask for an explanation.	☐ Do Activity 23, p. 323 as a writing activity. ☐ Do Activity 24, p. 324 as a writing activity. You write to the information center to get explanations on what each sign means. ☐ For additional practice, do Activities 4–5, p. 333 in the **Grammaire supplémentaire**. ☐ For additional practice, do Activity 10, p. 127 in the **Cahier d'activités**.
Study the **Vocabulaire** on page 324.	☐ Do Activity 26, p. 325 as a writing activity. ☐ For additional practice, do Activity 6, p. 334 in the **Grammaire supplémentaire** ☐ For additional practice, do Activities 5–9, pp. 98–100 in the **Travaux pratiques de grammaire**. ☐ For additional practice, do Activities 11–15, pp. 127–129 in the **Cahier d'activités**. ☐ For additional practice, do Activities 3–4, CD 3 in the **Interactive CD–ROM Tutor**.

Nom_____ Classe_____ Date_____

■ DEUXIEME ETAPE Student Make-Up Assignments Checklist
Pupil's Edition, pp. 326–327

Study the expressions in the **Comment dit–on...?** box on page 326: making observations; giving impressions. You should know how to make an observation and give an impression.

☐ Do Activity 30, p. 326 as a writing activity. Write six sentences using the expressions in the boxes.

☐ Do Activity 31, p. 327.

☐ Do Activity 32, p. 327.

☐ For additional practice, do Activities 8–10, pp. 334–335 in the **Grammaire supplémentaire.**

☐ For additional practice, do Activities 10–12, pp. 100–101 in the **Travaux pratiques de grammaire.**

☐ For additional practice, do Activities 16–17, p. 130 in the **Cahier d'activités.**

☐ For additional practice, do Activities 5–6, CD 3 in the **Interactive CD–ROM Tutor.**

CHAPITRE 11

■ DEUXIEME ETAPE Self-Test

Can you ask for explanations?	What would you say to ask…
	1. what something is?
	2. what something is called?
	3. what something means?
	4. what ingredients are in a dish?
	5. how to say something in French?
Can you make observations?	What observations would you make about…
	1. your town?
	2. your school?
	3. a place you visited?
	4. learning French?
Can you give impressions?	How would you give your impressions of these situations?
	1. people having fun dancing
	2. people looking bored at a birthday party
	3. a boy in a kayak paddling very fast with a crocodile following him

 For an online self-test, go to **go.hrw.com**.

WA3 FRANCOPHONE AMERICA–11

12 Echanges sportifs et culturels

■ PREMIÈRE ÉTAPE Student Make-Up Assignments Checklist

Pupil's Edition, pp. 345–347

Study the **Vocabulaire** on page 301.

- [ ] Do Activity 7, p. 346 as a writing activity. Match each item with its illustration, then write the sport it is associated with.

- [ ] Do Activity 8, p. 346 as a writing activity.

- [ ] Do Activity 9, p. 347 as a writing activity. Using the illustrations and the word box, write a conversation between you and a friend.

- [ ] For additional practice, do Activities 1–5, pp. 102–103 in **Travaux pratiques de grammaire.**

- [ ] For additional practice, do Activities 2–4, pp. 134–135 in the **Cahier d'activités.**

- [ ] For additional practice, do Activity 1, CD 3 in the **Interactive CD–ROM Tutor.**

■ PREMIERE ETAPE Student Make-Up Assignments Checklist

Pupil's Edition, pp. 348–349

<table>
<tr>
<td>Study the expressions in the Comment dit–on...? box on page 348: expressing anticipation; making suppositions; expressing certainty and doubt. You should know how to express anticipation, certainty and doubt. You should also know how to make a supposition.</td>
<td>

☐ For additional practice, do Activities 6–7, p. 136 in the **Cahier d'activités.**

☐ For additional practice, do Activity 2, CD 3 in the **Interactive CD–ROM Tutor.**

</td>
</tr>
<tr>
<td>Study the expressions in the Grammaire box on page 348: the future after quand and dès que.</td>
<td>

☐ Do Activity 13, p. 349.

☐ Do Activity 14, p. 349 as a writing activity.

☐ For additional practice, do Activities 2–5, pp. 360–361 in the **Grammaire supplémentaire.**

☐ For additional practice, do Activities 6–7, p. 104 in the **Travaux pratiques de grammaire.**

☐ For additional practice, do Activity 8, p. 137 in the **Cahier d'activités.**

☐ For additional practice, do Activity 3, CD 3 in the **Interactive CD–ROM Tutor.**

</td>
</tr>
</table>

■ PREMIERE ETAPE Self-Test

Can you express anticipation?	How would you express your anticipation if your were… 1. going to watch the Olympic games? 2. about to be an exchange student in Switzerland? 3. traveling to a foreign country?
Can you make suppositions?	What suppositions can you make about the following situations? 1. Your school team is going to compete in a state tournament. 2. You have to tell your best friend you've lost his or her leather jacket. 3. You're going to spend the summer working in a store.
Can you express certainty and doubt?	Your friend asks you the following questions. How would you express your certainty? 1. Est–ce que l'équipe de basket–ball américaine va gagner la médaille d'or? 2. Est–ce qu'il y a une interro de maths demain? 3. Est–ce que c'est une bonne idée d'étudier une langue étrangère? How would you express doubt about the situations above?

 For an online self-test, go to **go.hrw.com**.

WA3 FRANCOPHONE AMERICA–12

CHAPITRE 12

CHAPITRE 12

Echanges sportifs et culturels

■ DEUXIEME ETAPE Student Make-Up Assignments Checklist

Pupil's Edition, pp. 352–353

Study the **Vocabulaire** on page 352.	☐ Do Activity 22, p. 352 as a writing activity.
	☐ Do Activity 23, p. 353 as a writing activity. Write a conversation between you and your friend.
	☐ For additional practice, do Activities 6–8, pp. 362–363 in the **Grammaire supplémentaire**.
	☐ For additional practice, do Activities 8–13, pp. 105–107 in the **Travaux pratiques de grammaire**.
	☐ For additional practice, do Activity 11, p. 139 in the **Cahier d'activités**.
	☐ For additional practice, do Activity 4, CD 3 in the **Interactive CD–ROM Tutor**.
Study the expressions in the **Comment dit–on…?** box on page 353: inquiring. You should know to inquire about someone's country.	☐ Do Activity 25, p. 353 as a writing activity.
	☐ For additional practice, do Activities 12–13, pp. 140–141 in the **Cahier d'activités**.
	☐ For additional practice, do Activity 5, CD 3 in the **Interactive CD–ROM Tutor**.

CHAPITRE 12

Holt French 3 Allez, viens!, Chapter 12

■ DEUXIEME ETAPE Student Make-Up Assignments Checklist

Pupil's Edition, p. 355

Study the expressions in the **Comment dit–on...?** box on page 355: expressing excitement and disappointment. You should know how to express excitement and disappointment.

☐ Do Activity 29, p. 355 as a writing activity.

☐ For additional practice, do Activities 14–15, pp. 141–142 in the **Cahier d'activités.**

☐ For additional practice, do Activity 6, CD 3 in the **Interactive CD–ROM Tutor.**

CHAPITRE 12

■ DEUXIEME ETAPE Self-Test

Can you inquire?	You've just been introduces to an exchange student from a foreign country. What questions would you ask to find out...
	1. what life is like in that country?
	2. what people eat and wear there?
	3. what is typical there?
Can you express excitement and disappointment?	How would you express your excitement if...
	1. your school's basketball team won the state championship?
	2. you got a perfect grade on a very difficult test?
	3. you received a birthday card with $100 check in side?
	How would you express your disappointment if...
	1. you just missed first place in a competition?
	2. you arrived late and found that your friends had left without you?
	3. you received a lower grade than you had expected on a test?

 For an online self-test, go to **go.hrw.com**.

WA3 FRANCOPHONE AMERICA–12

CHAPITRE 12

Alternative Quizzes

Nom _____ Classe _____ Date _____

France, les régions

■ PREMIERE ETAPE

Alternative Quiz 1-1A

Maximum Score: 50/100

Grammar and Vocabulary

A. You and your friends are back to school after vacation. Match each question or statement in the left column with the logical response on the right. (10 points)

1. Qu'est-ce que tu deviens?
2. C'était comment?
3. Tu t'es bien amusé(e)?
4. Ça fait longtemps qu'on ne s'est pas vu?
5. Je suis contente de te revoir.

   a. Super!
   b. Ça fait quatre ans.
   c. Rien de spécial.
   d. Moi aussi.
   e. Non, je me suis ennuyé(e).

SCORE [ ]

B. Sylvie is writing to her friend Patrick about her vacation. Complete her letter with the **passé composé** of the verbs in parentheses. (22 points)

> Cher Patrick,
>
> Ça va? Mes vacances étaient super! D'abord je/j' (1) _____ (aller) rendre visite à mon oncle en Bretagne. Il habite à St Malo, donc bien sûr, nous (2) _____ (faire) le tour des remparts. Un jour, nous (3) _____ (prendre) l'autocar pour aller au Mont St Michel. Nous (4) _____ (visiter) l'abbaye, puis en descendant, je/j' (5) _____ (vouloir) aller trop vite, je/j' (6) _____ (rater) une marche et je/j' (7) _____ (tomber). Malheureusement, je/j' (8) _____ (se fouler) la cheville et je ne pouvais plus marcher. Mon oncle (9) _____ (devoir) me porter jusqu'à l'autocar! Une fois rentrée à la maison, je/j' (10) _____ (rester) au lit pendant deux jours!
>
> Et toi, tu (11) _____ (partir) en famille? Donne-moi de tes nouvelles.
>
> Sylvie

SCORE [ ]

Alternative Quiz 1-1A

C. Sylvie is asking Patrick about his vacation. Based on Patrick's responses, complete Sylvie's questions. Use the words in the box below more than once, if necessary. (6 points)

Quand	Quel temps	Où	Comment	Avec qui

1. _____ est-ce que tu est allé?
   Au bord de la mer.

2. _____ est-ce que tu y est allé?
   Fin juillet.

3. _____ est-ce que tu y est allé?
   Avec ma famille.

4. _____ est-ce que tu y est allé?
   En train.

5. _____ est-ce qu'il a fait?
   Très beau.

6. _____ est-ce que tu as dormi?
   A l'hôtel.

SCORE _____

D. Some teenagers are talking about where they used to go on vacation as children. Complete their sentences by putting the verbs in parentheses in the **imparfait**. (12 points)

1. Moi, j' _____ (aller) voir mes cousins. Ils

   _____ (être) super–sympas! Ils _____

   (habiter) au bord de la mer. On _____ (nager) souvent.

2. Mes sœurs et moi, nous _____ (partir) souvent en colonie de

   vacances. Nous _____ (adorer) les chevaux et nous

   _____ (faire) beaucoup d'équitation.

3. Ma famille et moi, nous _____ (aller) toujours à la montagne en

   hiver. Mes parents _____ (faire) du ski, mais moi je

   _____ (préférer) faire des bonhommes de neige!

4. Et toi et ta famille, qu'est-ce que vous _____ (faire)? Est-ce que

   vous _____ (aller) à la montagne ou à la mer?

SCORE _____

TOTAL SCORE _____ /50

France, les régions

■ DEUXIEME ETAPE

Maximum Score: 50/100

Grammar and Vocabulary

A. Complete the conversation between a waiter and a customer in a restaurant. (10 points)

LE SERVEUR **(1)** _____ ?
(Have you made your selection?)

LA CLIENTE Non, **(2)** _____ ? Qu'est-ce que vous
(I can't make up my mind)

recommandez comme **(3)** _____ ?
(appetizer)

LE SERVEUR **(4)** _____ est excellente!
(The plate of raw vegetables)

LA CLIENTE D'accord.

LE SERVEUR Et comme **(5)** _____ ?
(main dish)

LA CLIENTE **(6)** _____ **(7)** un _____ ,
(I would like)   *(steak with french fries)*

(8) _____ s'il vous plaît.
(rare)

LE SERVEUR Bon, d'accord. Et comme **(9)** _____ ?
(drink)

LA CLIENTE **(10)** _____ , s'il vous plaît.
(A mineral water)

LE SERVEUR Très bien.

SCORE ☐

Alternative Quiz 1-2A

B. You are creating a menu for your French class. Write three items for each category on the menu. (9 points)

Chez Christophe

Entrées	*Plats principaux*	*Desserts*
_____	_____	_____
_____	_____	_____
_____	_____	_____

SCORE [   ]

C. Stéphane's mother is missing a few items. Complete what she asks him to buy with the correct form of the partitive (**du, de la, de l', des**), the indefinite article (**un, une**), or with **de (d')**. (11 points)

Bon, d'abord, passe à l'épicerie pour prendre **(1)** _____ *oignons,* **(2)** _____ *haricots*

verts, **(3)** _____ *riz et* **(4)** _____ *eau minérale. Prends aussi* **(5)** _____ *confiture, mais*

ne prends pas **(6)** _____ *beurre, j'en ai assez. Ensuite, va à la boucherie-charcuterie, il me*

faut **(7)** _____ *jambon et* **(8)** _____ *poulet. Aussi, n'oublie pas de passer à la boulan-*

gerie pour acheter **(9)** _____ *douzaine de croissants. Ensuite, va à la pâtisserie pour acheter*

(10) _____ *tarte aux fraises et* **(11)** _____ *gâteau. Voilà, c'est tout, merci.*

SCORE [   ]

D. Write two ingredients necessary to make each of the items below. Name a different ingredient each time. Don't forget to include the partitive article! (20 points)

1. une assiette de crudités _____ _____

2. une assiette de charcuterie _____ _____

3. une tarte aux fruits _____ _____

4. des crêpes _____ _____

5. une pizza _____ _____

SCORE [   ]

TOTAL SCORE [   ] /50

2 Belgique, nous voilà!

■ PREMIERE ETAPE

Alternative Quiz 2-1A

Maximum Score: 50/100

Grammar and Vocabulary

A. You are getting directions to Liège. Complete the directions with the appropriate expression from the box. Use each expression only once. (16 points)

conduire	carrefour	panneau	pour	Continuez	Tournez	traverser	l'entrée

Alors, la route **(1)** _____ Liège… Suivez la N. 29. Vous allez

(2) _____ un village, puis vous allez voir un **(3)** _____

qui indique **(4)** _____ de l'autoroute. **(5)** _____

tout droit jusqu'au **(6)** _____ . **(7)** _____ à

gauche. Cette route va vous **(8)** _____ à Liège.

SCORE [   ]

B. You overhear these remarks at the service station. Complete each remark by selecting the appropriate expression from the right column. Use each one only once. (14 points)

_____ 1. Pourriez-vous nettoyer _____ ?

_____ 2. Vous pouvez mettre _____ dans les pneus?

_____ 3. Vous pouvez _____ les freins?

_____ 4. J'ai un pneu _____ .

_____ 5. Je peux changer le pneu. Où est _____ ?

_____ 6. Je suis tombé en _____ d'essence.

_____ 7. Faites _____ , s'il vous plaît.

a. la vidange

b. panne

c. de l'air

d. le pare-brise

e. la roue de secours

f. vérifier

g. le plein

h. crevé

SCORE [   ]

Alternative Quiz 2-1A

C. You are discussing driving habits with your friends. Complete the sentences with the appropriate form of the verb **conduire**. (14 points)

1. Les Parisiens _____ trop vite.

2. Je ne _____ jamais la voiture de mon père.

3. En Angleterre, on _____ à gauche.

4. Est-ce que vous _____ calmement?

5. Mon frère _____ quelquefois la voiture de ma mère.

6. Mon frère et moi, nous _____ prudemment.

7. Et toi, tu _____ comment?

SCORE [____]

D. Your older brother hires you to keep his car clean and the tank full of gasoline, the rest is done by the mechanic, but he is impatient! How would he tell you to do your tasks, how would he tell the mechanic. Use the logical expressions from the box and the **tu** form commands your brother would give you and the **vous** form commands he would give the mechanic. (6 points)

Se grouiller   Faire le plein   Se dépêcher
  Faire la vidange   Mettre de l'huile dans le moteur   Nettoyer le pare-brise

A toi	Au garagiste
_____	_____
_____	_____
_____	_____

SCORE [____]

TOTAL SCORE [____] /50

CHAPITRE
2 Belgique, nous voilà!

■ DEUXIEME ETAPE

Grammar and Vocabulary

A. Brigitte and her friends are giving their opinions on a new movie. Put their comments under the appropriate heading. (14 points)

> Ça m'ennuie.   Ça me branche!   C'est mortel!
>
> C'est marrant comme tout!   Ça me casse les pieds!   C'est fou!   C'est dingue!

ENTHUSIASM	BOREDOM
_____	_____
_____	_____
_____	_____

SCORE [ ]

B. Camille is getting ready to travel to Belgium. Sophie is helping her check that everything is ready. Complete her answers by replacing the underlined words with the appropriate pronouns. (24 points)

1. — Je t'ai donné ma carte de Bruxelles?

   — Oui, tu _____ _____ as donnée.

2. — Tu vas acheter des pralines pour ta petite amie?

   — Oui, je vais _____ _____ acheter.

3. — Tu vas rapporter des cadeaux pour tes parents?

   — Oui, je vais _____ _____ rapporter.

4. — Tu as demandé de l'argent à tes parents?

   — Oui, je _____ _____ ai demandé.

5. — Tu as emprunté la valise de ton frère?

   — Oui, je _____ _____ ai emprunté.

6. — Tu as donné le numéro de téléphone à tes parents?

   — Oui, je _____ _____ ai donné.

SCORE [ ]

CHAPITRE 2

Alternative Quiz 2-2A

C. Use the floor plans of the museum to complete the directions below using the expression provided. You will not use all the expressions. (12 points)

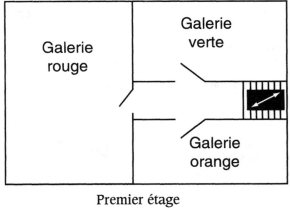

Premier étage

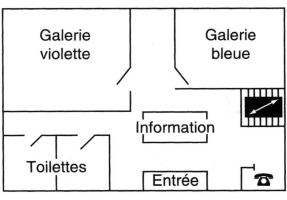

Rez-de-chaussée

à droite

à gauche

au bout

dans le coin

à côté

en face

en bas

en haut

— La Galerie verte n'est pas au rez-de-chaussée. Elle est (1) _____ ,

(2) _____ de la Galerie orange.

— La Galerie rouge est au premier étage, (3) _____ du couloir.

— Le téléphone est (4) _____ , (5) _____

de l'entrée.

— La Galerie orange est (6) _____ de l'escalier.

SCORE [____]

TOTAL SCORE [__/50]

CHAPITRE 2

Soyons responsables!

PREMIERE ETAPE

Grammar and Vocabulary

A. Brigitte is asking for permission to go out with her friends. Complete her requests with the appropriate expressions from the box below. (4 points)

Est-ce que je peux	Tu veux bien que	Ça te dérange	J'aimerais

1. _____ si j'invite des amis?

2. _____ j'aille au cinéma avec Sylvie cet après-midi?

3. _____ sortir avec Paul et Virginie ce soir?

4. _____ aller au concert jeudi.

SCORE [_____]

B. Brigitte's parents do not grant all of her requests. What do they say? (8 points)

1. _____ aujourd'hui.
   (It's not possible)

2. _____ .
   (OK, just this once)

3. _____ faire tes devoirs ce soir.
   (You must)

4. _____ sortir jeudi soir.
   (You're not allowed to)

SCORE [_____]

C. Your family has a very busy weekend. These are all the things you must do. Complete the sentences with the appropriate form of the verb **devoir**. (12 points)

1. Ton frère et toi, vous _____ écrire une lettre à vos grands-parents.

2. Mon père et moi, nous _____ nous occuper du jardin.

3. Je _____ faire la lessive.

4. Tu _____ t'occuper des animaux.

CHAPITRE 3

Alternative Quiz 3-1A

5. Tes frères _____ travailler samedi soir.

6. Ta sœur _____ s'entraîner pour son match de volley.

SCORE [   ]

D. Bertrand's mother is gone for the week and Bertrand is dividing up the household tasks among the other members of the family. Complete each statement with the appropriate verb. (10 points)

1. Caroline va...

_____ les feuilles

_____ la pelouse

_____ le jardin

2. Robert va...

_____ la lessive

_____ à manger au chat

_____ la table

3. Sylvie et moi, nous allons...

_____ les vitres

_____ la poussière

_____ l'aspirateur

_____ la salle de bains

SCORE [   ]

E. Bertrand's mother is coming back today but there's still work to do. Complete Bertrand's statements with the appropriate subjunctive forms of the verbs in parentheses. (16 points)

1. Il faut que nous _____ (être) responsables!

2. Et il faut que nous _____ (partager) les tâches ménagères!

3. Caroline et Robert, il faut que vous _____ (s'occuper) des enfants.

4. Il faut que les enfants _____ (sortir) le chien.

5. Sylvie, il faut que tu _____ (finir) de faire la vaisselle.

6. Moi, il faut que je _____ (faire) la cuisine.

7. Mais avant, il faut que je _____ (prendre) un aspirine parce que j'ai mal à la tête!

8. Caroline, il faut que tu _____ (venir) m'aider.

SCORE [   ]

TOTAL SCORE [/50]

CHAPITRE 3

3 Soyons responsables!

■ DEUXIEME ETAPE

Grammar and Vocabulary

A. Gilles is creating four signs to post around his neighborhood park. Help him write these signs by using different expressions for forbidding actions. (8 points)

    1. *It is forbidden to throw paper.*
    2. *Parking is not allowed.*
    3. *Please do not walk on the grass.*
    4. *No smoking.*

1. ☐

3. ☐

2. ☐

4. ☐

SCORE ☐

B. Complete the following list of what is good and bad for the environment. (24 points)

GOOD FOR THE ENVIRONMENT	BAD FOR THE ENVIRONMENT
_____ son véhicule	_____ du bruit
_____ le papier et le plastique	_____ l'énergie et l'eau
_____ un arbre	_____ des ordures dans l'eau
_____ les lumières	_____ des aérosols

SCORE ☐

CHAPITRE 3

Alternative Quiz 3-2A

C. You see a friend doing things you don't like. Reproach him for his behavior using the cues provided. (6 points)

1. _____ gaspiller l'eau.
   (You should not)

2. _____ cueillir des fleurs.
   (It's not good to)

3. _____ fumer.
   (You'd do well not to)

SCORE [   ]

D. As you reproach your friend, he justifies his actions. You, however, reject his excuses. Complete these conversations. Use different expressions for justifying actions and rejecting excuses each time. (12 points)

1. — Tu as tort de fumer.

   _____

   _____

   _____

   _____

   _____

2. — Tu as tort de cueillir des fleurs.

   _____

   _____

   _____

   _____

   _____

SCORE [   ]

TOTAL SCORE [   ] /50

CHAPITRE 3

Holt French 3 Allez, viens!, Chapter 3

4 Des goûts et des couleurs

Alternative Quiz 4-1A

Maximum Score: 50/100

■ PREMIÈRE ÉTAPE

Grammar and Vocabulary

A. A French friend is asking your opinion of the clothes some other friends are wearing. First, complete your friend's questions with the name of the indicated clothing item. Then give your opinion of the item. Use a different expression each time to state your opinion for each item. (16 points)

1. 2. 3. 4.

1. — Est-ce que tu aimes _____ de Pauline?

 — _____

2. — Regarde _____ de Jean-Claude. Il te plaît?

 — _____

3. — Comment tu trouves _____ de Pierre?

 — _____

4. — Et _____ de Caroline. Qu'en penses-tu?

 — _____

SCORE _____

B. Virginie is at a class reunion. Read her comments about the clothing she sees, and list the clothing items mentioned in the appropriate category. (16 points)

> Ce pantalon est trop sobre.
> Un costume comme celui-là, ça fait vieux!
> Quelles bottines géniales!
> Regarde ce sac! Il ringard, non!
> Cette chemise est vulgaire!
> Regarde la robe de Julie, quelle classe!
> Ces bottes sont tape-à-l'œil!
> Tu as vu le pendentif d'Elizabeth? Très élégant, non?

Alternative Quiz 4-1A

LIKES	DISLIKES
_____	_____
_____	_____
_____	_____
_____	_____
_____	_____
_____	_____

SCORE [____]

C. Sylvie and Fabienne are at the mall. They're talking about all the things they like. Complete their conversation with the appropriate forms of an interrogative or demonstrative pronoun. (18 points)

— Tu aimes ces bretelles?

— (1) _____ ? (2) _____ -ci?
       (Which ones)   *(These)*

— Comment tu trouves ce sac?

— (3) _____ ?
       (Which one)

— (4) _____ en cuir.
       (The one)

— Oh, regarde cette chemise! Comme elle est chic!

— (5) _____ ? (6) _____ en denim?
       (Which one)   *(The one)*

— Non, (7) _____ en soie.
           (The one)

— Et là, tu as vu ces hauts talons?

— (8) _____
       (Which ones)

— (9) _____ -là.
       (That one)

SCORE [____]

TOTAL SCORE [____] /50

4 Des goûts et des couleurs

■ DEUXIEME ETAPE

Alternative Quiz 4-2A

Maximum Score: 50/100

Grammar and Vocabulary

A. You're on your way to a party. Your friend is unsure about her appearance. Reassure her by paying her three different compliments. (9 points)

1. — Regarde ma nouvelle jupe. Tu ne la trouves pas un peu trop courte?

   — Mais non! _____ .

2. — Dis, je me suis fait teindre les cheveux. Ce n'est pas trop foncé?

   — Mais non! _____ .

3. — Je trouve que la couleur de ce chemisier ne me va pas très bien?

   — Au contraire! _____ .

SCORE ☐

B. How might your friend respond to the compliments given in Activity A? Use three different expressions to respond. (6 points)

1. _____

2. _____

3. _____

SCORE ☐

C. Several clients are getting their hair done today at the **Salon Dernière Mode.** Complete what each person says to the hairdresser by choosing the appropriate expression form the box. Use each expression only once. (15 points)

friser	teindre	raser	une coupe	un chignon
couper	la frange	une natte	une permanente

1. J'en ai marre d'avoir les cheveux raides. Je voudrais _____ .

2. J'ai les cheveux dans les yeux. Pourriez-vous me couper _____ .

Alternative Quiz 4-2A

3. Mes cheveux sont trops longs. J'ai besoin de/d' _____ .

4. Je n'aime plus la couleur de mes cheveux. Je voudrais me faire

   _____ les cheveux.

5. J'ai besoin de me _____ la barbe.

SCORE [ ]

D. You are a real "do-it-yourself," but your friend prefers to have everything done for him or her. What does your friend say in each case. Use the causative **faire**. (20 points)

1. — Je me fais une permanente moi-même.

   — Moi, je _____ chez le coiffeur.

2. — Je me coupe les cheveux moi-même.

   — Moi, je _____ chez le coiffeur.

3. — Je lave ma voiture moi-même.

   — Moi, je _____ par mon petit frère.

4. — Je change les pneus crevés moi-même.

   — Moi, je _____ par le garagiste.

5. — Je ramasse les feuilles du jardin moi-même.

   — Moi, je _____ par le fils du voisin.

SCORE [ ]

TOTAL SCORE [/50]

C'est notre avenir

PREMIERE ETAPE

Grammar and Vocabulary

A. Bertille is talking about what she and her friends plan for the future and on what these plans depend. Complete her statements with the appropriate present or future tense form of the logical verb. (24 points)

avoir	réussir	se marier	aller	pouvoir	obtenir	être	passer

— Si je/j' **(1)** _____ mon bac, j'irai à l'université.

— Si tu ne trouves pas de travail, tu **(2)** _____ au chômage.

— Si Janine trouve du travail, elle **(3)** _____ avec Pierre.

— Si Janine et Pierre se marient, ils **(4)** _____ des enfants.

— Si tu **(5)** _____ ton permis de conduire, tu

   (6) _____ acheter une voiture.

— Si nous **(7)** _____ notre diplôme, nous **(8)** _____

   aux Etats-Unis pendant les vacances.

SCORE _____

B. Ask a friend about her plans and say what you plan to do by putting the elements of these sentences in to a logical order. Don't forget the punctuation. (18 points)

1. faire / as / de / qu'est-ce que / tu / l'intention

   _____

2. mes / tiens / je / à / continuer / études

   _____

3. comptes / qu'est-ce que / tu / faire

   _____

4. de / il / médecine / études / possible / est / je / fasse / que / des

   _____

Alternative Quiz 5-1A

5. à / que / se peut / il / j'habite / Dakar

_____

6. me marier / pense / je

_____

SCORE [   ]

C. Marianne and Michel have the same plans for the future. However, while Marianne is very sure of what she is going to do, Michel is still unsure. Complete Michel's statements using either the future tense or the subjunctive as appropriate. (8 points)

1. MARIANNE   Je vais aller à l'université.

   MICHEL   Peut-être que j'_____ .

2. MARIANNE   Je vais faire des études de langues.

   MICHEL   Il est possible que je _____ .

3. MARIANNE   Je vais voyager.

   MICHEL   Peut-être que je _____ .

4. MARIANNE   Je vais trouver du travail à l'étranger.

   MICHEL   Il se peut que je _____ .

SCORE [   ]

TOTAL SCORE [   ] /50

CHAPITRE 5

CHAPITRE 5

C'est notre avenir

■ DEUXIEME ETAPE

Maximum Score: 50/100

Grammar and Vocabulary

A. You're not sure what you are going to do after high school. What are three ways you could answer this question to express you indecision? (9 points)

Tu sais ce que tu veux faire?

1. _____ .

2. _____ .

3. _____ .

SCORE [   ]

B. On the other hand, your friend, Hervé wants to be a pilot. What are three different ways he could complete these sentences. (6 points)

1. _____ être pilote.

2. _____ être pilote.

3. _____ être pilote.

SCORE [   ]

C. You're playing a game with your friends in which you have to guess what profession they are describing and complete their statements. (8 points)

1. Je m'appelle Gérard. Si vous avez mal aux dents, venez me voir parce que je suis

   _____ .

2. Je m'appelle Jason. J'adore les enfants. Je travaille dans une école. Je suis

   _____ .

3. Je m'appelle Caroline. J'adore écrire pendant des heures. Je voudrais écrire un roman. Je

   voudrais être _____ .

4. Je m'appelle Robert. Si vous avez une fuite d'eau dans la salle de bains ou dans la cuisine,

   appelez-moi parce que je suis _____ .

Student Make-Up Assignments **95**

CHAPITRE 5

Nom _____ Classe _____ Date _____

Alternative Quiz 5-2A

5. Je m'appelle Brigitte. J'adore les voitures. Si votre voiture est en panne, vous m'appelez parce que je suis _____ .

6. Je m'appelle Yves. J'adore conduire. Si vous avez besoin d'une limousine pour une occasion spéciale vous m'appelez parce que je suis _____ .

7. Je m'appelle Céline. J'adore les enfants, mais je ne les vois que lorsqu'ils sont malades. Je suis _____ .

8. Je m'appelle Jean-Luc. Je suis fort en maths, surtout en géométrie. Si vous cherchez la maison idéale, vous venez me demander d'en dessiner une. Je suis _____ .

SCORE _____

D. Brigitte is sure her life would be much better if only her high school days were over. Complete her journal entry with the conditional forms of the verbs in parentheses. (27 points)

Si j'avais mon bac, je/j' **(1)** _____ *(ne pas habiter)* avec mes parents.

Je/J' **(2)** _____ *(avoir)* un appartement. Je **(3)** _____ *(trouver)*

du travail. Le soir, je/j' **(4)** _____ *(aller)* voir mes amis, ou bien ils

(5) _____ *(venir)* chez moi. On **(6)** _____

(regarder) des films et on **(7)** _____ *(s'amuser)*. Pendant mes

vacances, mon amie Francine et moi, nous **(8)** _____ *(aller)* à

Tahiti. Je **(9)** _____ *(être)* heureuse.

SCORE _____

TOTAL SCORE _____ /50

Holt French 3 Allez, viens!, Chapter 5

6 Ma famille, mes copains et moi

PREMIERE ETAPE

Maximum Score: 50/100

Grammar and Vocabulary

A. Vincent has offended everyone today. Complete his apologies, as indicated. (10 points)

1. Je suis désolé d' _____ de te téléphoner.
   (to have forgotten)

2. Je suis désolé d' _____ en retard.
   (to have arrived)

3. Je suis désolé d' _____ ça.
   (to have said)

4. Je suis désolé de _____ à ta lettre.
   (to not have responded)

5. Je suis désolé d' _____ sans toi.
   (to have gone out)

SCORE [ ]

B. Laure and Vincent's love story starts out like that of many others. Complete the following account of what happens to them by filling in the blanks with the appropriate present tense of infinitive form of the verbs in parentheses. (18 points)

Laure se promène dans un parc et regarde les gens passer quand elle remarque un jeune

homme seul. Le jeune homme remarque aussi Laure. Les deux jeunes gens

(1) _____ *(se regarder)* pendant un moment, puis ils

(2) _____ *(se parler)* et ils (3) _____

(se donner) rendez-vous. Ils vont (4) _____ *(se retrouver)* au café.

Dès ce jour-là, ils (5) _____ *(se voir)* tous les jours. Il est évident

qu'ils (6) _____ *(s'aimer)*.

SCORE [ ]

Alternative Quiz 6-1A

C. You've lost your friend's favorite CD! Write three different expressions you could use to apologize for having lost the CD. Also, write three things your friend might say to accept your apologies. (12 points)

1. — _____ avoir perdu ton C.D.

— _____ .

2. — _____ avoir perdu ton C.D.

— _____ .

3. — _____ avoir perdu ton C.D.

— _____ .

SCORE [ ]

D. Two friends are making plans to get together. Complete their conversation according to the cues provided. (10 points)

— Ecoute, ça fait trop longtemps qu'on ne s'est pas vus!

(1) _____ ?
    (When are we getting together)

— Dis, **(2)** _____ visiter le nouveau musée? On pourrait
    (would you like to)
y aller demain après-midi.

— **(3)** _____ demain **(4)** _____ .
    (I'd like to, but)   *(I'm busy)*

— Alors, pourquoi pas aller au musée samedi?

— D'accord. **(5)** _____ ? On se retrouve devant le musée
    (How should we work this out)
vers une heure?

— D'accord. A samedi!

— Salut!

SCORE [ ]

TOTAL SCORE [/50]

CHAPITRE 6

Ma famille, mes copains et moi

■ DEUXIEME ETAPE

Grammar and Vocabulary

A. You're showing a family picture to a friend and explaining who everyone is. (24 points)

Tu sais, moi, j'ai une grande famille. Voilà une photo. Regarde, ça, c'est mon

(1) _____ , son **(2)** _____ est mort, donc
(great grand mother)   *(husband)*

elle est **(3)** _____ . Voilà mes tantes, les **(4)** _____
(widowed)   *(sisters)*

de mon père. Elles sont **(5)** _____ . Ma tante Christine est
(twins)

(6) _____ , mais ma tante Anne est **(7)** _____ .
(single)   *(married)*

Son **(8)** _____ a mon âge, on s'amuse bien ensemble. Et ça,
(son)

c'est mon frère **(9)** _____ . Il est **(10)** _____
(older)   *(divorced)*

et il a deux enfants. J'adore mon **(11)** _____ et ma
(nephew)

(12) _____ .
(niece)

SCORE [   ]

B. You are visiting a distant relative in Morocco for the first time. What might your host say in these situations? How would you respond? (16 points)

1. You host greets you and invites you in.

   — _____

   — _____

2. She offers you something to eat or drink.

   — _____

   — _____

Alternative Quiz 6-2A

3. She asks you if you would like some mint tea.

— _____

— _____

4. She thanks you for the flowers you brought.

— _____

— _____

SCORE [   ]

C. Stéphane and his little brother Etienne are always arguing. Finish what Stéphane says by selecting the appropriate option. (10 points)

1. ETIENNE   Stéphane, je peux jouer avec tes voitures?

   STEPHANE   Non, _____
   a. Tricheur!   **b.** Casse-toi!   **c.** Tant pis pour toi!

2. ETIENNE   Regarde ce que j'ai trouvé dans ta chambre! Des chocolats!

   STEPHANE   _____
   a. C'est toujours la même chose!   **b.** Tant pis pour toi!   **c.** Ne fouille pas dans mes affaires!

3. MAMAN   Etienne m'a dit que tu lui a donné un coup de pied. Il ne faut pas faire ça!

   STEPHANE   _____
   a. Casse-toi!   **b.** C'est lui qui a commencé!   **c.** Rapporteur!

4. ETIENNE   Stéphane a une petite amie… Stéphane a une petite amie…

   STEPHANE   _____
   a. C'est toujours moi qui prends!   **b.** Oh, ça va, hein?   **c.** Tant pis pour toi!

5. MAMAN   Stéphane, tu es le plus âgé, il faut que tu arrêtes de te disputer avec ton petit frère.

   STEPHANE   _____
   a. C'est toujours moi qui prends!   **b.** Oh, ça va, hein?   **c.** Tant pis pour toi!

SCORE [   ]

TOTAL SCORE [   ] /50

Nom _____ Classe _____ Date _____

Un safari-photo

■ PREMIÈRE ÉTAPE

Maximum Score: 50/100

Grammar and Vocabulary

A. The Zokoue family is deciding what to take with them on their safari. Complete these sentences by writing one logical thing they should take with them in each phrase. (16 points)

1. Pour se protéger les yeux du soleil, il faudra _____ .

2. S'il pleut, il faudra _____ .

3. En cas d'accident, il ne faudra pas oublier _____ .

4. Pour avoir de la lumière la nuit, il faudra _____ .

5. On veut prendre beaucoup de photos, donc il faudra _____ .

6. Comme il y a beaucoup de moustiques, il faudra _____ .

7. Comme nous allons à l'étranger, il faudra _____ .

8. Et pour toujours avoir à boire, il faudra _____ aussi.

SCORE ☐

B. You are going to Africa on a safari-photo. Name six different items you may see during your trip. (18 points)

_____

_____

_____

_____

_____

_____

SCORE ☐

Alternative Quiz 7-1A

C. Imagine that you are joining the Zokoues on their safari. How would you react if Lucie said these things to you? Give your reaction as shown in the example. (16 points)

Example: Je prendrai beaucoup de photos des animaux.
Je suis heureux (-euse) que tu prennes beaucoup de photos des animaux.

1. On fera faire nos passeports.

   Il est essentiel qu'on _____ .

2. Il faudra nous faire vacciner.

   Il est très important que nous _____ .

3. Nous verrons beaucoup d'animaux.

   Il se peut que nous _____ .

4. On goûtera des plats africains.

   Il faudrait que nous _____ .

5. Le voyage sera dangereux.

   Il est possible que le voyage _____ .

6. La nuit, il fera froid.

   La nuit, il se peut qu'il _____ .

7. Il y aura beaucoup de moustiques.

   J'ai peur qu'il _____ .

8. Nous nous amuserons bien!

   Il se peut que nous _____ .

SCORE _____

TOTAL SCORE _____ /50

CHAPITRE 7

Un safari-photo

■ DEUXIEME ETAPE

Maximum Score: 50/100

Grammar and Vocabulary

A. While at the zoo, Camille and her friends are talking about the animals that they see. Identify, in French, the animal that is being described. (14 points)

1. Regarde, là, c'est le roi des animaux! _____

2. Lui, il est très agile et il passe la plupart de son temps dans les arbres.

   _____

3. Regarde! On dirait un cheval rayé blanc et noir. _____

4. Comme elle est grande! Et regarde ce cou! _____

5. Lui, c'est l'animal le plus rapide. _____

6. Comme il est gros! Tu sais, il se sert de sa trompe pour boire!

   _____

7. Il a vraiment une bouche énorme! Tu sais qu'il passe pratiquement toute la journée dans

   l'eau? _____

SCORE [   ]

B. You're at the zoo. Express your astonishment at the different things you see using a variety of expressions. (15 points)

1. You see some very ferocious lions.

   _____

2. You see very mean elephant.

   _____

3. You see a shy antelope.

   _____

4. You see a very big gorilla.

   _____

Alternative Quiz 7-2A

5. You see beautiful butterflies.

_____

SCORE [   ]

C. Emile is talking with Marc about his new job: he will be working in a zoo over the summer. Complete their conversation with the subjunctive form of the verbs in parentheses. (21 points)

MARC   Dis donc! Tu vas travailler au zoo. Quelle chance!

EMILE   Oui, je commence ce soir. Tu sais, il est possible que ce

(1) _____ *(être)* dangereux. Il y a plein d'animaux

sauvages.

MARC   Des animaux sauvages, oui, bien sûr, mais ça m'étonnerait que tu

(2) _____ *(pouvoir)* les toucher. Mais il vaudrait mieux que

tu (3) _____ *(faire)* attention tout de même.

EMILE   Evidemment! Il faudra que je (4) _____ *(nettoyer)* les cages

tous les matins. Il sera essentiel que je (5) _____ *(être)* au

zoo de bonne heure.

MARC   J'ai peur que tu n'(6) _____ *(avoir)* pas beaucoup de

temps libre.

EMILE   Tu as raison. Bon, allez, il faut que j'(7) _____ *(aller)* au

travail. Salut!

SCORE [   ]

TOTAL SCORE [   ] /50

CHAPITRE 7

La Tunisie, pays de contrastes

■ PREMIERE ETAPE

Maximum Score: 50/100

Grammar and Vocabulary

A. Here's a list of some traditional Tunisian activities. Complete each logically. (21 points)

1. cultiver le _____

2. faire la _____ des figues

3. élever des _____ et des _____

4. donner à manger aux _____

5. _____ les vaches

6. faire de l' _____ (des bijoux, des objects en cuivre, etc.)

SCORE _____

B. You and some friends are speculating what you would do in different situations. Complete the statements with the appropriate imperfect or conditional form of the verbs in parentheses. (20 points)

1. Si j'allais en Tunisie, je _____ *(manger)* du couscous.

2. Si je _____ *(vouloir)* photographier des animaux sauvages, j'irais en Afrique.

3. Si je voulais acheter un tapis, j' _____ *(aller)* au Maroc.

4. Si j'allais au Maroc, je _____ *(boire)* du thé à la menthe.

5. Si c' _____ *(être)* possible, je visiterais le Texas.

6. Si je pouvais voyager, ce _____ *(être)* chouette!

7. Si je voyageais seule, mes parents _____ *(avoir)* peur.

8. Si j'allais en Suisse, je _____ *(faire)* du ski.

9. Si j'avais le choix, j' _____ *(habiter)* à la campagne.

10. Si j'avais le choix, je _____ *(préférer)* nager dans la mer.

SCORE _____

Alternative Quiz 8-1A

C. Your sister is going to visit an aunt you haven't seen in several months. Write three ways for
your sister to convey good wishes to your aunt. (9 points)

1. _____ .

2. _____ .

3. _____ .

SCORE [   ]

TOTAL SCORE [/50]

Holt French 3 Allez, viens!, Chapter 8

8 La Tunisie, pays de contrastes

■ DEUXIEME ETAPE

Alternative Quiz 8-2A

Maximum Score: 50/100

Grammar and Vocabulary

A. What other words can you use to say these things about city life? (12 points)

1. un endroit pour prendre le bus   un _____ de bus

2. l'air pollué qu'on respire en ville   la _____

3. plein de gens   la _____

4. des gens peu polis   des gens mal _____

5. des gens qui marchent vite   des gens _____

6. un passage pour traverser la rue à pied   un passage pour _____

SCORE [ ]

B. How do you think life in the country compares to life in the city? Make comparisons using the cues provided. (16 points)

1. (+ tranquille) La vie à la campagne est _____ la vie en ville.

2. (- chère) La vie à la campagne est _____ la vie en ville.

3. (- compliquée) La vie à la campagne est _____ la vie en ville.

4. (= sympa) La vie à la campagne est _____ la vie en ville.

5. (- voitures) Il y a _____ à la campagne qu'en ville.

6. (+ arbres) Il y a _____ à la campagne qu'en ville.

7. (= problèmes) Il y a _____ à la campagne qu'en ville.

8. (- stress) Il y a _____ à la campagne qu'en ville.

SCORE [ ]

Alternative Quiz 8-2A

C. Sylvie is telling you how life in the country differs from life in the city. Does she do the following things more, less, or as much? (8 points)

1. A la campagne, on marche _____ . (+)

2. A la campagne, on voit _____ souvent nos amis. (=)

3. A la campagne, on sort _____ . (-)

4. A la campagne, on étudie _____ . (=)

SCORE [   ]

D. Didier just moved to the city from the country, but he feels that everything is better in the country. Complete his statements with the appropriate French word for *better*. (14 points)

1. J'aime _____ habiter dans une petite ville.

2. L'air à la campagne est _____ .

3. On mange _____ à la campagne qu'en ville.

4. La circulation est _____ à la campagne.

5. Les promenades à pied sont _____ .

6. En général, je pense que la vie est _____ à la campagne!

7. Les gens vivent _____ à la campagne.

SCORE [   ]

TOTAL SCORE [   ] **/50**

CHAPITRE 8

9 C'est l'fun!

■ PREMIERE ETAPE

Maximum Score: 50/100

Grammar and Vocabulary

A. You're watching TV at your friend's house. Complete these statements made by various family members with the appropriate expression from the box below. (15 points)

> le programme télé   le son   un magnétoscope   la télécommande
>
> l'image   le téléviseur   une cassette vidéo

1. Je n'aime pas ce programme. Est-ce qu'on a _____ à regarder?

2. Voilà _____ . Il est tout neuf, avec un écran plus grand que le dernier.

3. Tu peux baisser _____ , s'il te plaît?

4. Je voudrais savoir ce qu'il y a à la télé. Où est _____ ?

5. Si Papa regarde la télé, c'est toujours lui qui a _____ .

SCORE _____

B. Based on what your friends say, suggest what they should watch on TV. (15 points)

1. — J'aime surtout les programmes sur les animaux.

   — Tu devrais regarder _____ .

2. — J'aimerais savoir ce qui se passe dans le monde.

   — Tu devrais regarder _____ .

3. — Quel temps va-t-il faire demain?

   — Tu devrais regarder _____ .

4. — J'adore la musique.

   — Tu devrais regarder _____ .

5. — J'aime beaucoup les bandes dessinées.

   — Tu devrais regarder _____ .

SCORE _____

❋ Alternative Quiz 9-1A

C. You are bored. You try to decide on something to do. Complete your monologue based on the cues provided. (20 points)

Je **(1)** _____ sais _____ quoi faire. **(2)** _____ est
(no longer) *(No one)*

à la maison… Pierre **(3)** _____ est _____ rentré du travail.
(not yet)

(4) _____ Etienne _____ Claude _____
(neither… nor) *(do not)*

répondent au téléphone. Il **(5)** _____ y a _____ à la télé. Bon,
(nothing)

alors je vais trouver un bon livre à lire!

SCORE [   ]

TOTAL SCORE [/50]

9 C'est l'fun!

■ DEUXIEME ETAPE

Alternative Quiz 9-2A

Maximum Score: 50/100

Grammar and Vocabulary

A. Béatrice is talking about some movies she has seen. Complete her statements with **qui, que,** or **dont.** (30 points)

1. C'est l'histoire d'un savant. Ce savant rencontre un homme _____ lui parle de ses expériences secrètes pour créer un être humain. Cet être humain est un monstre _____ personne n'aime alors le savant crée une compagne _____ ressemble au monstre. C'est un film génial!

2. C'est l'histoire d'une adolescente _____ est en vacances avec son père. Elle rencontre un garçon super-mignon et elle lui fait croire _____ son père est son petit ami. C'est vraiment marrant.

3. Ce film, _____ se passe pendant la Seconde Guerre mondiale, est l'histoire d'un homme juif _____ la famille est déportée. Il s'enfuit *(flees)* en France. Là, il rejoint *(joins)* un groupe de résistance _____ détruit *(destroys)* les chemins de fer.

4. C'est l'histoire d'un petit garçon _____ le père devient le Père Noël. Après plusieurs mois, il arrive à convaincre son père _____ il est vraiment le Père Noël et il l'aide à distribuer tous les cadeaux.

SCORE [ ]

B. What kinds of films did Béatrice see? Read the plots of the films in Activity A and identify the genre of each film. (8 points)

1. _____
2. _____
3. _____
4. _____

SCORE [ ]

CHAPITRE 9

Alternative Quiz 9-2A

C. Martine is talking to her friend about the movie she saw the previous evening. Complete their conversation using the cues provided. (12 points)

— J'ai été voir Sidekicks au cinéma hier soir.

— Ah, oui? **(1)** _____ ?
(What's it about)

— **(2)** _____ un garçon qui a des problèmes avec les
(It's about)
autres jeunes de son quartier.

— Où est-ce que **(3)** _____ ?
(...it take place)

— Aux Etats-Unis.

— **(4)** _____ ?
(How does it start)

— **(5)** _____ , il rencontre son idole dans ses rêves.
(At the beginning)

(6) _____ , il prend des leçons de karaté. Il y a
(At the end)
beaucoup d'action, c'est un très bon film.

SCORE [____]

TOTAL SCORE [____ /50]

10 Rencontres au soleil

Alternative Quiz 10-1A

■ PREMIERE ETAPE

Maximum Score: 50/100

Grammar and Vocabulary

A. You're creating a project about the sea life in the ocean. List, in French, five kinds of marine life that you might want to include in your presentation. (15 points)

1. _____

2. _____

3. _____

4. _____

5. _____

SCORE _____

B. Sylvie is telling Pascale who in her group of friends is good at certain things. Pascale responds by saying that someone else is the best in that area. Complete Pascale's remarks with the appropriate superlative form. (20 points)

— Il chante bien, Etienne.

— Oui, mais c'est Brigitte qui chante **(1)** _____ .

— Jean-Jacques et Marc sont très sportifs.

— Oui, mais Martine est **(2)** _____ du groupe.

— François parle très bien anglais.

— Oui, mais de nous tous, c'est Pierre qui parle anglais **(3)** _____ .

— André est très bon nageur, n'est-ce pas?

— Oui, mais Marcel est **(4)** _____ nageur du groupe.

— Et regarde Maxime, il est courageux, non?

— Oui, mais Edouard et Marc sont **(5)** _____ du groupe.

SCORE _____

Alternative Quiz 10-1A

C. How could you respond if a friend said these things to you? Choose the most appropriate response. (15 points)

_____ 1.

a. Oh, arrête de te vanter.

b. Ben, ça peut arriver à tout le monde.

c. Lâche-moi, tu veux?

_____ 2.

a. Oh, j'en ai vu d'autres.

b. Arrête de m'embêter!

c. Oh, ça va, hein?

_____ 3.

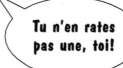

a. Alors là, tu m'épates!

b. Oh, j'en ai vu d'autres.

c. Ben, ça peut arriver à tout le monde.

_____ 4.

a. Alors là, tu m'épates!

b. Lâche-moi, tu veux?

c. Oh, j'en ai vu d'autres.

_____ 5.

a. Je t'ai pas demandé ton avis.

b. Alors là, tu m'épates!

c. Oh, ça va, hein?

SCORE _____

TOTAL SCORE _____ /50

CHAPITRE 10

CHAPITRE 10

10 Rencontres au soleil

■ DEUXIEME ETAPE

Grammar and Vocabulary

A. Bernard has just returned from his vacation. Much has happened in his absence and his friend Véronique is trying to fill him in. Every time Véronique starts to tell him something, Bernard interrupts to guess what has happened. Complete what Bernard says with a logical expression. (20 points)

Example: — Tu sais, Fabrice a emprunté la voiture de ses parents et devine…
— **Il a embouti leur voiture, n'est-ce pas?**

1. — Tu te souviens comme Ophélia a toujours aimé les boucles d'oreilles. Et bien…

   _____

2. — Tu savais que Julien et Anne s'aimaient, alors…

   _____

3. — Figure-toi que Robert est tombé de cheval, et…

   _____

4. — Tu te souviens comme Fabien ne conduisait pas bien du tout? Figure-toi que…

   _____

5. — Tu sais, Mireille et Thérèse ne se parlent plus parce que…

   _____

SCORE [   ]

B. Bernard's little brother told him what happened between Roméo and Juliette during his absence. Now Bernard is repeating the news to Véronique. Complete his statements with the appropriate past perfect forms of the verbs in parentheses. (15 points)

Mon frère m'a dit hier que Roméo et Juliette **(1)** _____

(se bagarrer). Apparemment, ils **(2)** _____ *(se donner)*

rendez-vous au café mais Roméo ne pouvait pas y aller. Juliette a attendu pendant une heure

parce qu'il **(3)** _____ *(oublier)* de lui téléphoner pour la

prévenir. Ensuite, Roméo **(4)** _____ *(se fâcher)* parce que

Alternative Quiz 10-2A

Juliette **(5)** _____ *(décider)* de casser. Mais finalement, Roméo lui a

demandé pardon et il lui a dit qu'il lui téléphonerait la prochaine fois.

SCORE [＿＿＿＿]

C. Now Véronique is telling Bernard about another friend. Tell what happened using the past perfect forms of the verbs in parentheses. (15 points)

On m'a dit que Béatrice **(1)** _____ *(partir)* en vacances au

bord de la mer et qu'elle **(2)** _____ *(tomber)* de cheval, qu'elle

(3) _____ *(se casser)* une jambe et qu'elle

(4) _____ *(aller)* à l'hôpital. Mais quand Béatrice est rentrée

de vacances, elle m'a dit qu'elle **(5)** _____ *(s'amuser)* !

SCORE [＿＿＿＿]

TOTAL SCORE [＿＿＿＿] /50

CHAPITRE 10

Laissez les bons temps rouler!

Maximum Score: 50/100

■ PREMIERE ETAPE

Grammar and Vocabulary

A. You're preparing a party. What are five types of music, in French, that you would consider playing at your party? (15 points)

1. _____
2. _____
3. _____
4. _____
5. _____

SCORE _____

B. Based on the types of music you listed in Activity A, name two instruments or types of equipment associated with each one. Do not repeat any items. (20 points)

1. _____
_____
2. _____
_____
3. _____
_____
4. _____
_____
5. _____
_____

SCORE _____

Alternative Quiz 11-1A

C. Vincent and Claire are talking about their tastes in music. Complete their conversation using the cues provided. (15 points)

— (1) _____ la musique classique?
         (What do you think of)

— Ça (2) _____ . Et toi?
            (I'm not into that)

   (3) _____ , la musique classique?
         (Do you like)

— Non! (4) _____ ?
            (Are you crazy or what)

   (5) _____ !
         (I never listen to it)

SCORE [   ]

TOTAL SCORE [/50   ]

Nom_____ Classe_____ Date_____

Laissez les bons temps rouler!

■ DEUXIEME ETAPE

Maximum Score: 50/100

Grammar and Vocabulary

A. Your French friend Janine is visiting you in Louisiana. She sees and hears many things she doesn't recognize. How would she asks you for an explanation of these things. (8 points)

1. Janine wants to know what "zydeco" means.

   _____

2. You're preparing gombo and Janine wants to know how it's made.

   _____

3. Janine wants to know where the word "Cajun" comes from.

   _____

4. You're preparing a sandwich and Janine wants to know what it's called.

   _____

   SCORE [_____]

B. Identify the Louisiana food specialty being described below. (8 points)

1. C'est une soupe dans laquelle il y a du riz, des okras et du crabe.

   _____

2. Ce sont des crustacés très épicés cuits au court-bouillon.

   _____

3. C'est un hors-d'œuvre cuit avec des épinards. Elles sont plus grosses qu'en France.

   _____

4. C'est un excellent dessert plein de raisins secs.

   _____

   SCORE [_____]

Alternative Quiz 11-2A

C. Janine is making observations and giving her impressions of different things in Louisiana. Using the clues provided, complete each observation or impression with a different aspect of Louisiana life. (24 points)

1. _____ , c'est _____ .
   (What scared me)

2. _____ , c'est _____ .
   (What catches your eye)

3. _____ , c'est _____ .
   (What I love)

4. _____ , les _____ .
   (They seem to like to dance)

SCORE [ ]

D. You are telling Janine about your favorite restaurant in New Orleans. Complete your statements with **ce qui** or **ce que**. (10 points)

(1) _____ me plaît, c'est le festival. Voilà (2) _____ on

peut y faire : écouter de la musique, manger de la cuisine cajun, danser.

(3) _____ on joue comme musique au festival, c'est de tous les genres,

mais (4) _____ je préfère, c'est le jazz. Et quand on a faim,

(5) _____ est très bon, c'est le po-boy!

SCORE [ ]

TOTAL SCORE [/50]

CHAPITRE 11

12 Echanges sportifs et culturels

Nom _____ Classe _____ Date _____

■ PREMIERE ETAPE

Grammar and Vocabulary

A. Identify in French, the sport being describe below. (20 points)

1. L'athlète se sert de rames. _____

2. L'athlète monte à cheval. _____

3. L'athlète saute à la perche. _____

4. L'athlète saute d'un plongeoir. _____

5. L'athlète se sert de barres asymétriques et d'anneaux. _____

SCORE [   ]

B. Sabine and her twin brother, Vincent, love water sports. She is dreaming about what they will soon do. Complete her statements with the future tense of the verbs in parentheses. (15 points)

1. Dès que les vacances _____ *(commencer)*, je partirai au lac avec ma famille.

2. Quand on _____ *(être)* au lac, je ferai du ski nautique.

3. Quand Vincent et moi _____ *(avoir)* 15 ans, nous apprendrons à plonger.

4. Quand nous _____ *(aller)* à la piscine, nous nous entraînerons.

5. Quand mes parents nous _____ *(voir)*, ils seront très contents.

SCORE [   ]

CHAPITRE 12

Alternative Quiz 12-1A

C. Vincent has doubts about his ability to dive. Complete Vincent's statements with the appropriate forms of the verbs in parentheses. (15 points)

1. Si j'étais plus agile, j' _____ *(avoir)* moins de difficultés à plonger.

2. Si le plongeoir était moins haut, je _____ *(pouvoir)* mieux plonger.

3. Si mes parents connaissaient mes difficultés, ils m' _____ *(encourager)*.

4. Si j'avais le courage, je leur _____ *(dire)* de venir me voir.

5. Si je pouvais m'entraîner plus souvent, je _____ *(faire)* plus de progrès.

SCORE [＿＿＿]

TOTAL SCORE [＿＿ /50]

12 Echanges sportifs et culturels

Nom _____ Classe _____ Date _____

■ DEUXIEME ETAPE

Maximum Score: 50/100

Grammar and Vocabulary

A. Several athletes at the Olympics are getting acquainted with each other. Complete their statements by saying where they come from. (20 points)

1. Je suis russe. Je _____ .

2. Et moi, je suis tunisien. Je _____ .

3. Voilà mon ami Ahmed. Il est algérien. Il _____ .

4. Kristof est allemand. Il _____ .

5. Ma sœur et moi, nous sommes américaines. Nous _____ .

6. Et vous deux, vous êtes anglais, n'est-ce pas? Vous _____ ?

7. Mes parents sont d'origines chinoises. Ils _____ .

8. Et toi? Tu es brésilien? Tu _____ ?

9. Christine est suisse. Elle _____ .

10. Et voilà Sylvie et Bertrand. Ils sont français. Ils _____ .

SCORE ☐

B. You're a young Olympics reporter, you've just met an athlete from a foreign country. First ask him where he is from. Then ask him four more questions about his country, such as what life is like, what one eats, what one wears, and what is found around there. (10 points)

1. _____

2. _____

3. _____

4. _____

5. _____

SCORE ☐

Alternative Quiz 12-2A

C. While reporting on the Olympics, you've made new friends. One of these new friends has invited you to come home with her to Sénégal and write about her country, all expenses paid! Make four statements to express your excitement to her. (20 points)

1. _____
2. _____
3. _____
4. _____

SCORE ☐

TOTAL SCORE ☐ /50

Answer Key

Answers to Alternative Quizzes 1-1A, 1-2A, 2-1A and 2-2A

Alternative Quiz 1-1A

A. (10 points; 2 points per item)
Possible answers:
1. c   3. e   5. d
2. a   4. b

B. (22 points; 2 points per item)
1. suis allée   7. suis tombée
2. avons fait   8. me suis foulé
3. avons pris   9. a dû
4. avons visité   10. suis restée
5. ai voulu   11. es parti
6. ai raté

C. (6 points; 1 point per item)
1. Où   4. Comment
2. Quand   5. Quel temps
3. Avec qui   6. Où

D. (12 points; 1 point per item)
1. allais; étaient; habitaient; nageait
2. partions; adorions; faisions
3. allions; faisaient; préférais
4. faisiez, alliez

Alternative Quiz 1-2A

A. (10 points; 1 point per item)
1. Vous avez choisi
2. je n'arrive pas à me décider
3. entrées
4. L'assiette de crudités
5. plat principal
6. J'aimerais
7. steak-frites
8. saignant
9. boisson
10. Une eau minérale

B. (9 points; 1 point per item)
Possible answers:
Entrées : jambon, assiette de crudités, carottes râpées
Plats principaux : steak, côtelettes de porc, filet de sole
Desserts : tarte aux fruits, gâteau, glace

C. (11 points; 1 point per item)
1. des   5. de la   9. une
2. des   6. de   10. une
3. du   7. du   11. un
4. de l'   8. un

D. (20 points; 2 points per item)
Possible answers:
1. des carottes, du vinaigre
2. du pâté, du jambon
3. des pommes, des fraises
4. du lait, du sucre
5. du fromage, des tomates

Answers Alternative Quiz 2-1A

A. (16 points; 2 points per item)
1. pour   5. Continuez
2. traverser   6. carrefour
3. panneau   7. Tournez
4. l'entrée   8. conduire

B. (14 points; 2 points per item)
1. d   5. e
2. c   6. b
3. f   7. g
4. h

C. (14 points; 2 points per item)
1. conduisent   5. conduit
2. conduis   6. conduisons
3. conduit   7. conduis
4. conduisez

D. (6 points; 1 point per item)
Possible answers:
A toi : Fais le plein! Nettoie le pare-brise! Grouille-toi!
Au garagiste : Faites la vidange! Mettez de l'huile dans le moteur! Dépêchez-vous!

Answers Alternative Quiz 2-2A

A. (14 points; 2 points per item)
ENTHUSIASM: Ça me branche! C'est dingue! C'est marrant comme tout! C'est fou!
BOREDOM: Ça me casse les pieds! Ça m'ennuie! C'est mortel!

B. (24 points; 2 points per pronoun)
1. me, l'   4. leur, en
2. lui, en   5. la, lui
3. leur, en   6. le, leur

C. (12 points; 2 points per item)
Possible answers:
1. en haut   4. dans le coin
2. en face   5. à droite
3. au bout   6. à gauche

Holt French 3 Allez, viens!

Student Make-Up Assignments **127**

Answers to Alternative Quizzes 3-1A, 3-2A, 4-1A and 4-2A

Alternative Quiz 3-1A

A. (4 points; 1 point per item)
1. Ça te dérange
2. Tu veux bien que
3. Est-ce que je peux
4. J'aimerais

B. (8 points; 2 points per item)
1. Ce n'est pas possible
2. Ça va pour cette fois
3. Tu dois
4. Tu n'as pas le droit de

C. (12 points; 2 points per item)
1. devez 3. dois 5. doivent
2. devons 4. dois 6. doit

D. (10 points; 1 point per item)
Caroline va...: ramasser, tondre, arroser
Robert va...: faire, donner, mettre
Sylvie et moi, nous allons...: laver, faire, passer, nettoyer

E. (16 points; 2 points per item)
1. soyons 5. finisses
2. partagions 6. fasse
3. vous occupiez 7. prenne
4. sortent 8. viennes

Alternative Quiz 3-2A

A. (8 points; 2 points per item)
Possible answers:
1. Il est interdit de jeter des papiers
2. Interdiction de stationner
3. Veuillez ne pas marcher sur la pelouse
4. Interdiction de fumer

B. (24 points; 3 points per item)
GOOD FOR THE ENVIRONMENT:
partager, recycler, planter, éteindre
BAD FOR THE ENVIRONMENT: faire, gaspiller, jeter, utiliser

C. (6 points; 2 points per item)
1. Tu ne devrais pas
2. Ce n'est pas bien de
3. Tu ferais mieux de ne pas

D. (12 points; 6 points per item)
Possible answers:
1. — Je suis quand même libre, non?
   — Ce n'est pas une raison.

2. — Je ne suis pas le seul à cueillir des fleurs.
   — Ce n'est pas parce que tout le monde le fait que tu dois le faire.

Answers Alternative Quiz 4-1A

A. (16 points; 4 points per item)
Possible answers:
1. le caleçon; Je le trouve super!
2. le gilet; Non, il ne me plaît pas du tout!
3. la cravate; Je l'aime bien.
4. la mini-jupe; Je la trouve tape-à-l'œil.

B. (16 points; 2 points per item)
LIKE: les bottines, la robe, le pendentif
DISLIKES: le pantalon, les bottes, la chemise, le sac, le costume

C. (18 points; 2 points per item)
1. Lesquelles 6. Celle
2. Celles 7. Celle
3. Lequel 8. Lesquels
4. Celui 9. Ceux
5. Laquelle

Answers Alternative Quiz 4-2A

A. (9 points; 3 points per item)
Possible answers:
1. Elle te va comme un gant.
2. Ça fait très bien.
3. Ça va avec tes yeux.

B. (6 points; 2 points per item)
Possible answers:
1. Tu crois?
2. Ça te plaît vraiment?
3. C'est gentil.

C. (15 points; 3 points per item)
1. une permanente 4. teindre
2. la frange 5. raser
3. une coupe

D. (20 points; 4 points per item)
Possible answers:
1. me fais faire une permanente
2. me fais couper les cheveux
3. fais laver ma voiture
4. fais changer les pneus crevés
5. fais ramasser les feuilles du jardin

ANSWERS

Answers to Alternative Quizzes 5-1A, 5-2A, 6-1A and 6-2A

Alternative Quiz 5-1A

A. (24 points; 3 points per item)
1. réussis
2. seras
3. se mariera
4. auront
5. passes
6. pourras
7. obtenons
8. irons

B. (18 points; 3 points per item)
1. Qu'est-ce que tu as l'intention de faire?
2. Je tiens à continuer mes études.
3. Qu'est-ce que tu comptes faire?
4. Il est possible je fasse des études de médecine.
5. Il se peut que j'habite à Dakar.
6. Je pense me marier.

C. (8 points; 2 points per item)
1. irai à l'université
2. fasse des études de langues
3. voyagerai
4. trouve du travail à l'étranger

Alternative Quiz 5-2A

A. (9 points; 3 points per item)
Possible answers:
1. Pas vraiment.
2. Non, je n'ai aucune idée.
3. Non, je me demande...

B. (6 points; 2 points per item)
Possible answers:
1. Je voudrais
2. Mon rêve, c'est d'
3. Ce qui me plairait, c'est d'

C. (8 points; 1 point per item)
1. dentiste
2. instituteur
3. écrivain
4. plombier
5. mécanicienne
6. chauffeur
7. médecin
8. architecte

D. (27 points; 3 points per item)
1. n'habiterais pas
2. aurais
3. trouverais
4. irais
5. viendraient
6. regarderait
7. s'amuserait
8. irions
9. serais

Answers Alternative Quiz 6-1A

A. (10 points; 2 points per item)
1. avoir oublié
2. être arrivé
3. avoir dit
4. ne pas avoir répondu
5. être sorti

B. (18 points; 3 points per item)
1. se regardent
2. se parlent
3. se donnent
4. se retrouver
5. se voient
6. s'aiment

C. (12 points; 2 points per item)
Possible answers:
1. — Je m'excuse d'
   — Ce n'est pas grave.
2. — Pardonne-moi d'
   — Ne t'inquiète pas.
3. — Je suis vraiment désolé(e) d'
   — Ça arrive à tout le monde.

D. (10 points; 2 points per item)
1. Quand est-ce qu'on se revoit
2. ça te plairait de
3. J'aimerais bien mais
4. je suis pris(e)
5. Comment est-ce qu'on fait

Answers Alternative Quiz 6-2A

A. (24 points; 2 points per item)
1. arrière-grand-mère
2. mari
3. veuve
4. sœurs
5. jumelles
6. célibataire
7. mariée
8. fils
9. aîné
10. divorcé
11. neveu
12. nièce

B. (16 points; 2 points per item)
Possible answers:
1. — Bonjour, entrez. Asseyez-vous.
   — Vous êtes bien aimable.
2. — Je vous sers quelque chose?
   — Je prendrais bien du thé.
3. — Vous désirez du thé à la menthe?
   — Oui, merci.
4. — Merci bien. C'est vraiment gentil de votre part.
   — Je vous en prie.

C. (10 points; 2 points per item)
1. b   2. c   3. b   4. b   5. a

Holt French 3 Allez, viens!

Student Make-Up Assignments **129**

ANSWERS

Answers to Alternative Quizzes 7-1A, 7-2A, 8-1A and 8-2A

Alternative Quiz 7-1A

A. (16 points; 2 points per item)
Possible answers:
1. des lunettes de soleil / un chapeau
2. un imperméable / un parapluie
3. une trousse de premiers soins / des pansements / un désinfectant
4. une torche
5. un appareil-photo / des pellicules
6. de la lotion anti-moustique
7. un passeport / des chèques de voyage
8. une gourde

B. (18 points; 3 points per item)
Answers may vary.

C. (16 points; 2 points per item)
1. fasse faire nos passeports
2. nous fassions vacciner
3. voyions beaucoup d'animaux
4. goûtions des plats africains.
5. soit dangereux
6. fasse froid
7. ait beaucoup de moustiques
8. nous amusions bien

Alternative Quiz 7-2A

A. (14 points; 2 points per item)
1. le lion
2. le singe
3. le zèbre
4. la girafe
5. le guépard
6. l'éléphant
7. l'hippopotame

B. (15 points; 3 points per item)
Possible answers:
1. C'est fou comme ils sont féroces, ces lions!
2. Qu'est-ce qu'il est méchant, cet éléphant!
3. Tu as vu comme elle est timide, l'antilope?
4. Je n'ai jamais vu un aussi gros gorille.
5. Quels beaux papillons!

C. (21 points; 3 points per item)
1. soit
2. puisses
3. fasses
4. nettoie
5. sois
6. aies
7. aille

Answers Alternative Quiz 8-1A

A. (21 points; 3 points per item)
1. blé
2. cueillette
3. *any two:* chameaux, moutons, chèvres
4. *any one:* poules, chameaux, moutons, chèvres
5. traire
6. artisanat

B. (20 points; 2 points per item)
1. mangerais
2. voulais
3. irais
4. boirais
5. était
6. serait
7. auraient
8. ferais
9. habiterais
10. préférerais

C. (9 points; 3 points per item)
Possible answers:
1. Embrasse-la pour moi.
2. Dis-lui que je vais lui écrire.
3. Dis-lui que je pense à elle.

Answers Alternative Quiz 8-2A

A. (12 points; 2 points per item)
1. arrêt
2. pollution
3. foule
4. élevés
5. pressés
6. piétons

B. (16 points; 2 points per item)
1. plus tranquille que
2. moins chère que
3. moins compliquée que
4. aussi sympa que
5. moins de voitures
6. plus d'arbres
7. autant de problèmes
8. moins de stress

C. (8 points; 2 points per item)
1. plus
2. aussi
3. moins
4. autant

D. (14 points; 2 points per item)
1. mieux
2. meilleur
3. mieux
4. meilleure
5. meilleures
6. meilleure
7. mieux

Answers to Alternative Quizzes 9-1A, 9-2A, 10-1A and 10-2A

Answers Alternative Quiz 9-1A

A. (15 points; 3 points per item)
1. une cassette vidéo
2. le téléviseur
3. le son
4. le programme télé
5. la télécommande

B. (15 points; 3 points per item)
1. un documentaire
2. les informations
3. la météo
4. un vidéoclip
5. un dessin animé

C. (20 points; 4 points per item)
1. ne... plus
2. personne n'
3. n'... pas encore
4. ni... ni... ne
5. n'... rien

Answers Alternative Quiz 9-2A

A. (30 points; 3 points per item)
1. qui, que, qui
2. qui, que
3. qui, dont, qui
4. dont, qu'

B. (8 points; 2 points per item)
Possible answers:
1. un film de science-fiction / un film d'horreur
2. une comédie / un film d'amour
3. un film de guerre / un film historique / un drame
4. une comédie

C. (12 points; 2 points per item)
Possible answers:
1. De quoi ça parle
2. Ça parle d' / C'est l'histoire d' / Il s'agit d'
3. ça se passe
4. Comment est-ce que ça commence
5. Au début
6. A la fin

Answers Alternative Quiz 10-1A

A. (15 points; 3 points per item)
Possible answers:
1. des requins
2. des crevettes
3. des pieuvres
4. du corail
5. des homards

B. (20 points; 4 points per item)
1. le mieux
2. la plus sportive
3. le mieux
4. le meilleur
5. les plus courageux

C. (15 points; 3 points per item)
1. a
2. a
3. c
4. b
5. c

Answers Alternative Quiz 10-2A

A. (20 points; 4 points per item)
Possible answers:
1. Elle s'est fait percer les oreilles, n'est-ce pas?
2. Ils se sont fiancés, n'est-ce pas?
3. Il s'est fait mal au dos, n'est-ce pas?
4. Il a pris des leçons de conduite, n'est-ce pas?
5. Elles se sont bagarrées à cause de Philippe, n'est-ce pas?

B. (15 points; 3 points per item)
1. s'étaient bagarrés
2. s'étaient donné
3. avait oublié
4. s'était fâché
5. avait décidé

C. (15 points; 3 points per item)
1. était partie
2. était tombée
3. s'était cassé
4. était allée
5. s'était amusée

Answers to Alternative Quizzes 11-1A, 11-2A, 12-1A and 12-2A

Answers Alternative Quiz 11-1A

A. (15 points; 3 points per item)
Possible answers: *Any five of:*
le rock, la musique cajun, la musique classique, le blues, le jazz, le country, le rap, la dance, la pop

B. (20 points; 2 points per item)
Possible answers: *Any ten of:*
la batterie, la guitare, l'accordéon, la flûte, le piano, le saxophone, la trompette, la basse, la boîte à rythmes, le synthé, le micro

C. (15 points; 3 points per item)
1. Qu'est-ce que tu penses de
2. ne me branche pas trop
3. Ça te plaît
4. Tu délires ou quoi
5. Je n'écoute jamais ça

Answers Alternative Quiz 11-2A

A. (8 points; 2 points per item)
1. Qu'est-ce que ça veut dire, «zydeco»?
2. Comment est-ce qu'on fait le gombo?
3. D'où vient le mot «cajun»?
4. Comment est-ce qu'on appelle ce sandwich?

B. (8 points; 2 points per item)
1. du gombo
2. des écrevices
3. des huitres Rockefeller
4. du pouding au pain

C. (24 points; 3 points per item)
Possible answers:
1. Ce qui m'a fait peur, c'est l'alligator.
2. Ce qui saute aux yeux, c'est les couleurs des masques.
3. Ce que j'aime / j'adore, c'est la musique cajun.
4. Ils ont l'air d'aimer danser, les cajuns.

D. (10 points; 2 points per item)
1. Ce qui
2. ce qu'
3. Ce qu'
4. ce que
5. ce qui

Answers Alternative Quiz 12-1A

A. (20 points; 4 points per item)
1. l'aviron
2. l'équitation
3. l'athlétisme
4. le plongeon acrobatique
5. la gymnastique

B. (15 points; 3 points per item)
1. commenceront
2. sera
3. aurons
4. irons
5. verront

C. (15 points; 3 points per item)
1. aurais
2. pourrais
3. encourageraient
4. dirais
5. ferais

Answers Alternative Quiz 12-2A

A. (20 points; 2 points per item)
1. viens de Russie
2. viens de Tunisie
3. vient d'Algérie
4. vient d'Allemagne
5. venons des Etats-Unis
6. venez d'Angleterre
7. viennent de Chine
8. viens du Brésil
9. vient de Suisse
10. viennent de France.

B. (10 points; 2 points per item)
Possible answers:
1. Tu es d'où?
2. C'est comment, la vie là-bas?
3. Qu'est-ce qu'on y mange?
4. Qu'est-ce qu'on porte chez toi?
5. Qu'est-ce qui est typique chez toi?

C. (20 points; 5 points per item)
Possible answers:
1. Génial!
2. C'est trop cool!
3. J'arrive pas à y croire!
4. C'est pas possible!